JOSHUA DAVIES

Why Do I Matter?

FINDING YOUR IDENTITY IN CHRIST

ISBN: 9798322414179

Cover design by Brad Barker (www.bradbarker.design).

TABLE OF CONTENTS

DEDICATION

To my beautiful wife and kids who always support me.
I love you. You mean more to me than anything in this world.
You are my world and I love being your Husband and Father.

INTRODUCTION

*G*rowing up, my parents were foster parents. I'm not going to lie; I wasn't a fan. In my brief understanding of fostering, I knew we would get kids who would come live with us. Sometimes they weren't so lovely. Some I liked, others I couldn't stand. Ok, saying I couldn't stand them is probably harsh, let us go with I wasn't a fan. One because they were mean or two, because we just didn't click. Some were my age, some were older, some were younger, and it felt like we never knew how they would react to us as a family. One day Zach, who would run away any chance he got, went berserk while we were camping as a family. He started flinging his arms, throwing anything he could find, and my dad, a big dude (he looked like Stone Cold Steve Austin in my mind), bear-hugged him and carried him back to our camper.

I saw the love my father had for these foster kids. It was at that moment I finally got it. Why did my parents go through the hurt and pain of fostering? I could see their discomfort and pain because having a kid leave was always hard on them. They poured so much of themselves into these kids. For them, it was pure joy. They loved these kids just like they loved their biological children, and it didn't matter if they were the meanest or the worst of the bunch. They loved them like their own.

I was about thirteen when Tanya came to live with us. She was 16, and I thought it was cool to have an older sister. We would hang out, listen to music and make my parents' lives miserable. Just kidding. Well, for the most part. I was only in seventh grade, but she made me feel more incredible than I actually was. We were both in youth group, so I hung around her friends like the annoying little brother I was.

She was the first to treat all of us like family. It wasn't hard to love her like a sister; to this day, I still talk about her to people like she is. She had a family a few hours from where we lived, and when she turned 18, she ran away to go be with them. I felt betrayed. I felt abandoned. I couldn't imagine how my parents felt. She had been with us for almost two years. But that's life as a foster parent.

Next up was my baby sister Rachel. She's honestly the real reason I wrote this book. She was just 2 years old when she came to live with us. She had been abandoned by her parents and left in her crib for the first 2 years of her life. It was a heartbreaking story. She was in respite with a family only an hour from where we lived at the time. We got her for a weekend to see how it would work out, and we instantly fell in love with her. We knew we were the perfect fit for her. So, we sent her back to her respite family, and in four weeks we would become her permanent home. However, there was a fire in her home just a few days later. Everyone was able to escape on their own but her. She was trapped in her crib and had to be rescued through her window. So, we got her 2 weeks earlier than we were supposed to. Can I pause here to tell you a story of how Holy Spirit works in our lives?

Rachel was about 6, and we were at a 4th July gathering
with friends who lived near where she was in respite care.
To preface this story, the doctors said Rachel would never
walk. Ok, now we can continue… she's 6. A man walks
toward our group, and Rachel takes off after him. My
parents are flipping out, trying to stand up quick enough to
grab her. She jumps into this man's arms, and he utters the
words Rachel, it's so good to see you. Come to find out, this
was the fireman who pulled her out of the fire when she was
2 years old. My parents got to thank the man that saved their
daughter. It was such a fantastic moment.

Why do I keep bringing up the foster kids we had growing
up? A chapter in this book is called The Adopted One, and
there's a reason my baby sister sparked my imagination to
write this book. When she was four years old, my parents
were able to adopt her. The adoption process in America
is long and tedious. They persevered and got to name her
Rachel Amber Davies after the judge presiding over the case
deemed them fit to be her parents. I was 15 when we adopted
Rachel. I was overjoyed, and I could see my parents were
as well.

Being a foster kid can sometimes bring along identity issues
but who are we kidding, anything in life can bring on identity
issues. For me it was a traumatic experience from when I was
13 - 17 and again when I was 30. Identity crises don't care
if you're four or a hundred and four, whether you're just a

baby or you're older than Methuselah. Had to slide in a Bible joke somewhere. Identity is at the base of who we are. When we don't know who we are, the enemy can attack very easily. Look at Adam and Eve. When the enemy deceived Eve it was before she had a name, before she had an identity. Until they ate the fruit she is only known as woman. Adam then names her Eve because she will be the mother of all life. Not having an identity can open us up to all types of deceit and hurt. So how do we get an identity? How do we find our identity in Christ? We start with understanding everything we should identify as based on what God calls us.

As we dive into this book, we're going to look at all the ways God sees us, even if you don't feel that way right now, it doesn't mean He doesn't see you that way. Because he does. He's the Master Writer, the Master Artist, the Master Creator and the best Friend we could ever have.

CHAPTER ONE

The Adopted One

*Y*ou matter because of who God calls you. And God has adopted us into His family and calls you an adopted child of God. You matter to God. Adoption is funny to me because you don't just happen upon it. It's not like, oh, this kid lives with us now. Let's make it official and adopt them. You don't stumble into the process. It's so long and tedious that an average person would give up. You have to choose to love the child you are adopting. You have to choose to go through the hard work and jump through the bureaucratic red tape. You choose to make this person a part of your family. That's what the Apostle Paul means in Galatians when he says that God has adopted us into his family. When God says he adopted you into His family, He's saying He has chosen to love you! He has chosen you!

Adopted children become heirs to their parents' fortune or lack thereof. I kid, I kid. Our Heavenly Father has made you an heir by adopting you into His family. Romans says we have become heirs with Christ. Take a look at Galatians 4:4-7 and see how much God loves you.

> *"But when the right time came, God sent his Son, born of a woman, subject to the law. God sent him to buy freedom for us who were slaves to the law so that he could adopt us as his very own children. And because we are his children, God has sent the Spirit of his Son into our hearts, prompting us to call out, "Abba, Father." Now, you are no longer a slave but God's own child. And since you are his child, God has made you his heir." Galatians 4:4-7 NLT*

Adopted kids are chosen kids, and YOU have been chosen by God. We must learn our identity in Christ as adopted children. So many people put their identity in different baskets. Because at a very young age, it's taught to us to not put all of our eggs in one basket. But identity is different. You have to put all your eggs in one basket, and that basket is Jesus. So many times though we allow outer worldly things to shape who we are and we put our identity eggs in different baskets.

BASKET CASE

Not really but its a funny title. We can sometimes feel like a basket case when there's so many baskets containing our identity. It's scary really to be pulled in so many different directions wearing different baskets all the time. One for work, one for home, one for church, and one for your friends. What if you wore your work basket to church, or better yet your friends basket home. Would people recognize you as the person they thought you were? When your identity is in Jesus there are no different baskets to worry about, you understand you're an Adopted Child of God, you're Loved Unconditionally, you're God's Friend, you're a Masterpiece, you are Fearfully and Wonderfully Made, you are Created, you are Gifted, you're an Heir, you are Redeemed, you are Forgiven, you are Free. We don't always understand all that right from the start so, let's take a look at some of the baskets we allow to shape us.

ADOPTED KIDS ARE CHOSEN KIDS, AND YOU HAVE BEEN CHOSEN BY GOD.

1. WORK

Work! The number one thing people tend to throw themselves into when they don't have an identity. They will bring work home usually causing their spouse and kids to miss out on time with them. Or even worse, they will spend all their time at the office, maybe coming home for dinner but right back to the office as soon as they're done.

I remember growing up my dad had two jobs. He worked a full-time job during the day and at night he did his pastoral duties. He came home for dinner most nights, but he would be at the church right after. The only time I got to spend with him was if I went to church with him which I grew to love. But the point is work even when ministry can become our identity.

That's a scary place to be when your ministry becomes your identity. Whether you're the lead pastor, an associate pastor or just a lay person serving a role in the church it can be very easy for that role to become who you think you are. Your calling is not your identity. God is!

2. HOLLYWOOD

I love this one. We can put our identity in God on the back burner and be what Hollywood says we should be. You're not skinny enough. You're not as good looking as you need to be. Hollywood puts unhealthy ideas in our head of what we should be and who we should be.

Movies and TV Shows are so unrealistic when it comes to identity. The character is made by a writer. They're created from their imagination. Wait that sounds an awful lot like someone we've been talking about. The writer of the universe. The creator of everything and everyone. Just like a character is created by a writer out of their imagination you were created by the master writer out of His imagination in His image. Watching TV and movies can shape us not because they're trying to take over our minds, but because we can fall in love with a character and begin to emulate them.

Just know you are chosen by God and there is nothing greater than that.

One of my favorite movies of all time is Aladdin. And not because he lies to get what he wants but because he makes a promise to the genie that with his last wish he will set him free. And spoiler alert he keeps that promise. It shows character, it shows that he knows who he is. That he doesn't need that third wish to make him rich or a prince. But he uses it to set his friend free. God wants to set you free of your identity crisis and accept you into his family as an adoptive son or daughter.

3. PEOPLE, PLACES, THINGS

People make it easy to put our identity into them, we have our friend groups, our work colleagues, and our families. Spending time with people can shape who we become. Let's look at our friend groups. I had a group of friends growing up that I allowed to define who I was. If we're not careful we can start to identify ourselves just like our friends do instead of being the unique child of God we were made to be. If I watch certain preachers too long, I will begin to emulate them or copy their speech and mannerisms. It's just who we are. We're built to emulate those around us, it's how we fit in to certain clicks or church groups. But we have to remember we are an adopted child of God, and our identity is in Him.

Places, oh so many places in this world to fall in love with. We can put our identity in places because we love going there. Or we hate going there, like work, I kid, I kid. I love going to Disney World and it's easy for me to become a Disney fanatic and make that my identity because we go one to two times a year. A particular Winston Churchill quote is often-cited — "We shape our buildings; thereafter they shape us" — and the point it makes of buildings can equally be made of cities, neighborhoods or places.

Sometimes it's hard to place a finger on it but our homes or the places where we spend the most time can shape who we are. But we must remember we are chosen. And not just chosen but we are an adopted child of God. We can't allow places to shape who we are; we must put our identity eggs in Jesus rather than places.

GOD DIDN'T JUST PLUCK YOU FROM DUST, HE BREATHED LIFE INTO YOU AND CALLED YOU CHOSEN.

Imagine for a second that we allow the things we own and buy to shape who we really are. This kinda reminds me of a story in the Bible called the Rich Young Ruler. In short Jesus felt genuine love for him and told him to sell all of his possessions and follow him for he would have treasures in heaven. But the rich young ruler walked away sad for he had many possessions. I'm not saying it's not ok to have nice things. Surely if you have the financial freedom to have them, go for it. What I am saying is don't let your possessions shape who you are.

There's a TV show my wife and I like to watch together and

one of the main characters is fairly wealthy. He sometimes uses his wealth to gain things in life. But like the age-old song goes you can't get to heaven on roller skates. Nothing we have on this earth is coming with us to Heaven. No matter how much you try, it's not coming.

> *"Don't store up treasures here on earth, where moths eat them and rust destroys them, and where thieves break in and steal. Store your treasures in heaven, where moths and rust cannot destroy, and thieves do not break in and steal. Wherever your treasure is, there the desires of your heart will also be."*
> *Matthew 6:19-21 NLT*

4. FAMILY

Family is a big one. We can sometimes put all of our eggs in this basket. Because they mean so much to us. But they can hurt us pretty bad if we're not careful. Causing a shift and possibly even an identity crisis. Family can be a good basket too, just not for your identity.

Stay at home parents can get lost in the mundane of taking care of the kids and taking care of the house that they can lose track of whose they are. Kids in foster care or even those adopted can put their identity in their new family because someone finally loves them. And that's where the family basket can become bad when we forget that we are adopted by God and we are in His family and He calls us chosen one.

CHOSEN ONE

Chosen can be a funny word. From I am the chosen one to I was chosen last in dodge ball. But in everything that we can possibly use the word chosen for, you must remember you are the chosen one to God.

> *"You did not choose Me but I chose you, and appointed you that you would go and bear fruit, and that your fruit would remain, so that whatever you ask of the Father in My name He may give to you." John 15:16 NIV*

Like my parents chose to adopt my sister we are chosen adopted sons and daughters of God. God didn't just pluck you from dust, he breathed life into you and called you chosen. Even though you may have slipped up in your life or cussed someone out, he chose you. We don't choose God, like it says in John 15:16 He chooses us. I can remember standing in the courthouse with my siblings waiting for the verdict whether the judge was going to allow my parents to adopt Rachel. And then it finally came, the moment everyone anticipated. Rachel was now adopted by my parents and the rest of our family. You see we chose to love her. When you're blood they feel an obligation to love but when you're adopted they chose to love you. How does God choose to love us? It's all throughout the Bible really. From cover to cover it is a love story of a God who loves, it may be a jealous love at times, but it is love none the less.

WHY DO I MATTER?

This might have seemed like a weird chapter, but it was all about identity. And being an adopted child of God brings about our identity. I have a tattoo on my left arm that says adopted and written inside of it is the main verse in this chapter (Galatians 4:4-7). Its a beautiful verse telling us how he has adopted us into his family and we now cry out Abba Father. You matter because adopted kids are chosen kids.

You matter because you are the chosen one Luke Skywalker. I'm kidding but you seriously are chosen. *"For you did not choose me but I chose you."* is written in John 15:16. He chooses you, He, being God. That's why you matter so much. Because you are chosen. I'll say it one more time for the people in the back, adopted kids are chosen kids and you have been adopted into God's family.

REFLECTION

What does it mean to you when we say God adopted you into His family?

_____

_____

_____

_____

_____

_____

_____

_____

CHAPTER TWO

Where's The Love?

We all want to be loved, and much like the commercial known all over the world. "Where's the Beef?" "Where's the Love?" In the Old Testament, where's the love? I'm serious. We hear about this loving God who never changes in the New Testament. Still, all we see in the Old Testament is famine, destruction, and everything that doesn't fit the role of love as we know it. But the English language only has one word for love. So, what do we know about it? That's a different book entirely.

There is always an easy answer, but the easy answer is never good enough. The easy answer is to read Song of Songs, and you'll have all the love you need for the entire Bible. But amidst all of the captivity, destruction of cities, and even the "world" at one point, where is it? It's hard to see, but it's there, I promise. Have you ever been jealous? I'm serious; it's okay to answer - this is a safe place. I have been jealous before; my jealousy comes from the fear of being replaced. It happens more than I'd care to admit. Why am I talking about jealousy? Well, let's look at the Bible for this answer.

> *"You must worship no other gods, for the LORD, whose very name is Jealous, is a God who is jealous about his relationship with you." Exodus 34:14 NLT*

So, I ask again, where is the love? I hear questions all the time. If God is love, how could he destroy an entire civilization or flatten cities in the Old Testament?

TO GOD, IT'S NOT RECKLESS OR JEALOUS BUT, COMPLETELY CALCULATED.

To me, Exodus 34:14 makes the answer very clear. Jealousy. God destroyed the world with the flood because no one was worshiping him. Look at Nineveh. God sent a messenger (We won't get into the entire story here) to tell them they would be destroyed, and when they turned from their wicked ways and worshiped God, He spared them. There was a new relationship with God. I don't know about you, but jealousy has driven me to do some crazy things (I'm not saying they were or weren't justified). But if God is a jealous God, then in this imperfect person's opinion, a jealous love is the only thing that makes sense. So, where's the love? It's throughout the Old Testament in every decision, every act, and every miracle performed.

Is that answer sufficient? I only ask because the song Reckless Love caused a lot of controversies between Christians. Some said God couldn't be reckless. Others feel we shouldn't use that word to describe such Holiness. However, bear with me for a moment. Allow me to indulge in the wording. We use words today that would cause past generations to turn over in their grave. We have slang words that use words like bad to mean good all in the way it's used. One of my favorites is asking Holy Spirit to wreck a situation in my life, to flip it on its head, and to wreck it. Some people felt my using the word wreck was disrespectful. Much like people think the word reckless or jealous is disrespectful. What if we thought of it like this? To God, it's not reckless or jealous but, completely calculated. However, we do not understand what it means to be God or see things as he sees them. So to us, a simple explanation is his jealous/reckless love makes sense. To me, this is what that song is about. God's love is so big he would flatten a city to get to you. Where do you stand? Where's the love?

A NEW KIND OF LOVE

I started this chapter off the way I did because we need to understand God's love for us. But there is a new kind of love. Asking "Where's the love?" was playful yet symbolic of a fundamental question of where's the love outside Song of

Songs, Proverbs, and Psalms. This new love is found in the New Testament.

> *"For this is how God loved the world: He gave his one and only Son, so that everyone who believes in him will not perish but have eternal life. God sent his Son into the world not to judge the world, but to save the world through him."*
> *John 3:16-17 NLT*

You are so loved God sent down his only Son to earth for you. It's a new kind of love. A new covenant, a new set of rules, a new character in this story called life, and a Helper soon after His death. That Helper we call Holy Spirit. This is all part of the love that God has for you. So let's break this down:

He cares about you so much that He sent His Son to earth to die for the sins of the world. Including yours. Jesus said that the greatest commandments are to love the Lord God with all of your heart, soul, mind and strength and love your neighbor as yourself. God sent Holy Spirit to earth to dwell inside of you.

The new covenant is all about love. A love we may never understand but love all the less.

LOVE YOUR NEIGHBOR

Love your neighbor. That's a tough task. Why? Because the full statement is to love your neighbor as yourself. That last part is where it gets so tough. Most people reading this

book struggling with their identity don't view themselves as someone worthy of being loved. Some people hate or if hate is too strong a word, they really, really don't like themselves. So how could they possibly know how to love others?
I have a friend who is constantly saying, "God made me who I am, so deal with it." But I don't believe that's what God wants for us. I believe He wants us to come to love ourselves and the proof is in the verse James 2:8

> *"If you really keep the royal law found in Scripture, "Love your neighbor as yourself," you are doing right." James 2:8 NIV*

It's not love you for who you are, it's love you in spite of who you are. Romans 5:8 NLT states *"But God showed his great love for us by sending Christ to die for us while we were still sinners."* Because if I can love you as I love myself or as Christ loves me and I truly love myself, then it doesn't matter who you are, what your sin is, I will love you. God already loves us. We are His children.

> *"See what great love the Father has lavished on us, that we should be called children of God! And that is what we are! The reason the world does not know us is that it did not know him." 1 John 3:1 NIV*

It's hard for a world that does not truly understand love to understand why we love them. Why we love them had been a secret for many years. This big secret was something that was hidden from past generations. Paul reveals to us this big secret in Colossians. But I can ruin it before we read it. The big secret is that Christ came for us all. Every single person on this earth He came, He died, and He rose again for you, for me, for the saved and unsaved alike. For everyone.

THE BIG SECRET

> *"This message was kept secret for centuries and generations past, but now it has been revealed to God's people. For God wanted them to know that the riches and glory of Christ are for you Gentiles, too. And this is the secret: Christ lives in you. This gives you assurance of sharing his glory."*
> Colossians 1:26-27 NLT

IT'S NOT LOVE YOU FOR WHO YOU ARE, IT'S LOVE YOU IN SPITE OF WHO YOU ARE.

There was this big secret. Some translations call it a mystery. But when Paul reveals the big secret in Colossians 1:27, it's a revelation to many that this Jesus character didn't just die and resurrect for the Jews. That He did it all for everyone in this world. That His Helper was for everyone. Holy Spirit wasn't just for a select few 100-plus people in a room on the day of Pentecost. But for everyone in the world. That is why Jesus tells his disciples to go into all nations. He didn't say stay in Israel. The message was authentic and raw. Peter even witnessed the first gentile receive the baptism in Holy Spirit. The BIG secret was simple. It wasn't anything majestic in nature but a simple statement Christ lives in you. Boom!
Rock the nations!

WHY DO I MATTER?

You matter because of love. God loves you so much that He once sent His Son to die on the cross and take away all our sins. There was a big secret to say I love you. We are basically Gentiles and the big secret revealed is that Jesus came for all Jews and Gentiles. I would suggest if you haven't given your heart to Jesus yet, you put down this book and ask Him to come into your life and forgive you of your sins. That's how much he loves you that he would do that for you. You matter because God calls you loved.

<u>REFLECTION</u>

Being loved by our Heavenly Father can be tough for some when their earthly father wasn't the greatest. How does God's love make you feel?

_____

_____

_____

_____

_____

_____

_____

_____

CHAPTER THREE

A Holy Friend Zone

*N*ormally being in the "Friend Zone" is a bad thing for the person interested in someone but with God not so much. With God, you want to be in the "Friend Zone" rather let's call it "The Holy Friend Zone." Because with God the friend zone is safe, it's peaceful, and there are no expectations other than being friends.

I was crazy about a girl in high school that came to my church. Until one day she introduced me to some of her friends as her "Brother in Christ". I know what you're thinking, you've done that once or twice. I'm even guilty of introducing a girl as my "Sister in Christ" but it's an instant "Friend Zone." Once you're in the friend zone there's no expectations except to be a good friend. How do you do that?

You sit and listen, you learn about them. You learn what they like and what they don't like. You bring them a coffee every now and again. Or if you're me and don't like coffee it's an iced vanilla chai tea latte, please. God calls us Friend. You matter to God! Friendships are one of the greatest things we can have and a friendship with God is the same. It's special, it's one of those things we tend to take for granted, because He's just always been there for us.

I remember the first time I met one of my best friends. We didn't know much about each other, really, we didn't know anything about each other. I was leading worship at a church when he walked in. That first Friday he was there, I immediately introduced myself to him. I knew his name, and that was about it. We live in a small town in Wyoming, so it's nice to meet new people. Remember, though, we didn't know anything about each other.

ONCE YOU'RE IN THE FRIEND ZONE THERE'S NO EXPECTATIONS EXCEPT TO BE A GOOD FRIEND.

This is like our first encounter with God, isn't it? We don't really know much about Him. We see what others have said about Him. Sometimes good, sometimes bad, but we don't really know much. I began to learn more about my new friend over time. I learned that he had just gotten out of jail, which could be enough to send most people running, but I was intrigued. Why would the first place he wanted to go when he got out be church? It's like God. The bad people say about Him makes people want to run as far away from Him as possible, but the good intrigues us. I was intrigued by my new friend. I started to learn a little more about him, just like when we dig into God's Word, we know a little more about His heart. Instead of listening to what others say about Him, we begin to learn for ourselves.

FRIEND OF GOD

> *"You are my friends if you do what I command. I no longer call you slaves, because a master doesn't confide in his slaves. Now you are my friends, since I have told you everything the Father told me." John 15:14-15 NLT*

God calls us a friend in the verse above. We confide in our friends. Like we confide in our friends, we confide in God, but more importantly, He confides in us. That's how we make it through life.

> *"The LORD confides in those who fear Him; He makes His covenant known to them." Psalm 25:14 NIV*

What is fear first off? How can it be defined? I would define fear as an emotional response to something dangerous or out of our control. There's nothing dangerous about God. There's nothing about him that's out of our control. We get to love God, and He loves us back. We have free will to choose to do that. So why does this verse and seemingly every Pentecostal church I went to growing up always say to fear the Lord when fear is an emotional

response to something out of our control? The answer
is humility.

HUMILITY IN GOD

Humility is actually straightforward. We are called to humble
ourselves. This means recognizing that we are not perfect and
that we are in need of God's grace and mercy. We must be
willing to admit our weaknesses and shortcomings and seek
God's help to overcome them. The problem lies in the thin
line between humility and false humility. False humility brings
about a dangerous attitude to a situation. If you struggle with
false humility, you struggle with your identity in Christ. The
line is a fine one, a fragile line between the two, and with
that, it's easy to fall into false humility. When leading worship
and someone paid me a compliment, I always brushed it off
and said, oh, it was all Holy Spirit. See, this is precisely what
I am talking about. That's the fine line I was talking about. I
didn't mean to show false humility but brushing someone off
like that is exactly what I was doing. God gave me my talents
and abilities, so now I simply say thank you and move on.
However, to fear something brings about humility. Fear brings
us back down to earth. If we didn't have our fears, we would
emotionally be at the center of the universe. So, to fear the
Lord is to become humble before him.

Let's talk about humility for a second. So, what does humility
look like in ministry or everyday life? I can tell you this, I
saw a group of pastors at a men's retreat one weekend show

me what it was like to be humble before God. After being on the worship team all weekend, I cleaned off the stage and gathered my gear. Someone yelled we need to vacuum the sanctuary. This group of pastors stuck out to me because they were the first to grab a vacuum. Without hesitation, they plugged it in and began vacuuming. This struck me because many of us would instead be talking with our friends or lining up to take a picture with that weekend's speaker, but this group of pastors jumped up and said I'll do the hard work. Humility, in a worldly sense, looks different for everyone. Still, humility before God almost looks the same from person to person. What does that mean, really? Humility before God is basically submission to God and the things God finds good. Servanthood is a form of humility. It is very humbling as a pastor when you're cleaning bathrooms. Can I get an amen?

THE DRUM SET IN THE LIVING ROOM

My best friend, it's fun to say, but how do you get to that point? It wasn't like we were best friends overnight. I wanted to learn things about him. He wanted to learn something about me. It's much like God, where we need to know things about Him to grow in our relationship, and He wants to learn things about us. It's what friends do. We went on trips together, sometimes to the middle of nowhere, to pick up a drum set that he'd set up in his living room (that's for another time). Oh, you want to hear that story? Ok, so the drum set in the living room is funny to most people because when I had the privilege of marrying my best friend and his fabulous bride, the drum set in the living room made it into their vows.

His bride hated the drum set in the living room but he was learning to play the drums so he could be on the worship team at our church. So she put up with it even though tripping over it became the new norm and it blocking the tv became a possibility when he was sitting at it.

Have you ever been to small-town America? No? Well, let me try and paint a picture for you. It was a windy, hot day in Wyoming when I got a call that a drum set was for sale in South Dakota, and he was on his way to pick me up. According to the population sign getting off the interstate, our old town is the third-largest in Wyoming, with roughly 30,000 people. If you ask, google it is 32,857, so not bad. The smallest town I've been to, I don't know if it has a population, but Bill, WY, consists of a hotel, a diner, a post office, and a daycare that looks like a toy graveyard. I say this to explain the difference between Gillette and the nameless town in South Dakota.

If you blink, you have already driven through it, but he wanted this drum set. So we hop in his truck and head down the dirt roads to nowheresville, South Dakota. It gave us some time to talk as it was a four-hour drive round trip. He shared stories from his past, and I did the same, and we realized we had similar but very different histories. So we are supposed to meet the drum set people at a specific gas station. We can't find it, and we've driven through the town 10 times searching for it. Turns out it used to be a gas station, and they had the pumps taken out, but everyone still calls it the gas station. We get the drum set and start our drive back, sharing stories and life experiences. I would share some stories, but my best friend might kill me.

I will share that we went to a church conference one year and we wanted him to go, so I made a deal with the church that I would pay his way without him knowing. But when we checked into our hotel, they had tide pods right above a sign that said snacks. This was smack dab in the middle of the big let's eat tide pods

WE ARE IN UNITY WITH GOD WHEN WE PRAY.

craze. But my best friend notices it right away and points it out, and everyone with us is basically rolling on the floor. I don't mean like the Pentecostals we are. I mean, gut-laughing hysterics because my best friend made a tide pod joke while checking into the hotel. It's just the kind of guy he is, he's the life of the party, and it ain't over till he says it is. Laughing our way through small-town America. This is how friendships go. We learn about each other, and the same thing goes with God. It is so important we learn about God and also understand that God wants to learn about us. Even though he knows everything He still wants to know about you, He wants to hear it from you. He wants you to confide in Him.

HOW DO WE LEARN ABOUT GOD?

You could probably answer this question on your own. However, I truly believe we learn about God in three ways. The first way is through His living Word. I say living Word because I learn something new every time I open my Bible, and it's the churchy thing to say. The second is talking to Holy Spirit and listening for Him to talk back. Talkback? Yeah, talkback! Holy Spirit wants to speak to you. He wants to commune with you and confide in you. We learned that a couple pages back. The third is that He wants us to worship Him; we know the Father's heart through worship. Worship is one of those things where we think it's just singing songs on a Sunday morning. Really though, it is a lifestyle. If we want to drill down to the nitty-gritty, reading the Word and prayer are acts of worship.

There are so many different ways to read the Bible. Not one way will be perfect for you. Reading God's Word is an act of worship essential to learning the heart of the Father. Here are some ways I would suggest reading your Bible. A couple chapters a day, this works great for most people. You can read a couple chapters and journal about what stood out to you that day. I recently heard of a great idea to read the Bible. Read until you learn something, then write that truth down. The conference speaker who shared this direction stated he once found 21 truths in one chapter of the Bible. Next, we must learn to speak to God and hear His voice.

There are many different ways to pray and speak to Holy Spirit. We all pray and talk to Holy Spirit uniquely in our own way. But did you know that Jesus is praying for you too? As friends pray for each other, Jesus prayed for us on earth, and He prayed for all believers in John 17.

> *"My prayer is not for them alone. I pray also for those who will believe in me through their message, that all of them may be one, Father, just as you are in me and I am in you. May they also be in us so that the world may believe that you have sent me. I have given them the glory that you gave me, that they may be one as we are one— I in them and you in me—so that they may be brought to complete unity. Then the world will know that you sent me and have loved them even as you have loved me." John 17:20-23 NIV*

We are in unity with God when we pray. The most important part of prayer is that we learn to hear Holy Spirit as much as we learn to speak to Him. His voice is unique, and we can learn to decipher it from our own. I once had a friend say to me if you're learning to decipher the voice of Holy Spirit, do this. If the voice says something good, it is most likely Holy Spirit because we are not inherently good. Our thoughts are not always, "Hey, I should pray for this lady's neck." In my belief, that's Holy Spirit 99% of the time. Prayer in and of itself is an act of worship.

Worship is so many things to so many people. What is worship to you, and what does it look like? Is it singing songs, praising the Father's name, or lifting your hands in surrender to God? Raising my hands used to be a funny thing, and even when I lead worship, I put them more out to the side than up in the air. I don't know why, but I do. It just feels more comfortable for me. I hated it when worship leaders or preachers said, "lift your hands to the Lord." As a worship leader and pastor, I find myself doing the very same thing. It's easy to want people to worship, but we also must understand that everyone worships in their own way. It may not look like raising your hands to the Lord in surrender. They may worship with their hands in their pockets. It's still worship because worship isn't just singing songs, lifting our hands, hanging from the chandeliers, rolling around on the ground, or running across the tops of pews. It's living every day reading your Bible, conversing with Holy Spirit, and singing some songs to worship the King of Kings.

Best Friends and a relationship with God are very similar. We confide in each other, spend time with each other, and have conversations while driving down the road. It might sound weird, but I talk to Holy Spirit daily while driving in a quiet car or if I can't figure out a problem at work. I know He's there listening, and just like a best friend, He wants to learn about me just like I want to learn about Him.

WHY DO I MATTER?

God calls you friend. Friendships are special in multiple ways. You can confide in a friend. Friends can confide in you and God does confide in you, we discussed this earlier. But the most important aspect of being friends with God is He already knows everything about you and yet yearns for us to know him on new levels. You matter and you are a friend to God. Sometimes you have to put your metaphorical drum set in your living room and rock out. There's this drummer I like to watch in videos. He's a heavy metal drummer who does funny videos of playing heavy metal drums to worship songs. Why did I tell you that story because sometimes we do out of the box things to learn about an out of the box God who calls us friend. You matter! God calls you friend. Join "The Holy Friend Zone."

REFLECTION

We talked a lot about friendships. How does knowing God calls you a friend help shape your identity?

_____

_____

_____

_____

_____

_____

_____

_____

CHAPTER FOUR

Masterpiece of Perfection

y favorite saying when discussing this topic is the following. A masterpiece is still a masterpiece even when it's covered up. I know that phrase may not make sense, so bear with me. Let's take the Mona Lisa, yes, National treasure style. But seriously, think of the Mona Lisa. Now take a bunch of mud and compost and spread it all over the painting. Now think to yourself. Underneath all that mud and leaves is still a masterpiece. God calls us a masterpiece in Ephesians 2:10.

> *"For we are God's masterpiece. He has created us anew in Christ Jesus, so we can do the good things he planned for us long ago." Ephesians 2:10 NLT*

We cover that masterpiece with sin, doubt and fear, but underneath is still the masterpiece God created. So a masterpiece is still a masterpiece even when it's covered up. I love that phrase. I once preached this as a sermon and bought a lion painting from Family Dollar. During the sermon, I covered it with shaving cream. I also took a knife and made cuts and holes in it. As I preached bit by bit, I scraped off the shaving cream revealing the masterpiece painted in 2022 by Family Dollar. At the end of the sermon, I pulled out a second painting. Identical to the one I just cut up and sprayed shaving cream on. This one was perfect, and that's how God sees us. We often look at the junk in our lives, not the masterpiece underneath it. So you pile more garbage on. You say to yourself, it's ok if you do more drugs, watch more porn, tell that little white lie that "won't" hurt anyone, or drink a fifth of Jack because you call yourself worthless, when God calls you a masterpiece. Did you know that Ephesians 1 states that God loved you so much that he knew what you would do before creating the world and still chose to adopt you into his family? That's something I have trouble wrapping my mind around. Don't believe me? Read it for yourself...

> *"Even before he made the world, God loved us and chose us in Christ to be holy and without fault in his eyes. God decided in advance to adopt us into his own family by bringing us to himself through Jesus Christ. This is what he wanted to do, and it gave him great pleasure." Ephesians 1: 4-5 NLT*

TOO MUCH JUNK IN YOUR TRUNK

We have all sinned and fallen short of the glory of God, but that's where grace comes in. Grace can be tricky, though, because Romans 5 tells us where sin abounds, grace abounds more, but Romans 6 tells us not to use that as an excuse to keep sinning. So there's a balance. We need to repent, which means turning away from our sin. How do we do that? How can we just up and quit our sin? With the help of Holy Spirit, for one. Secondly, with the help of our friends and loved ones. Let's talk about porn addiction for a second. Seconds up, next topic. I'm just kidding, this is very serious, and I can't say enough how much I've watched porn ruin marriages. It's not something to take lightly. My dad's fall from ministry started with porn addiction, which became several emotional affairs over Yahoo Instant Messenger. That ultimately became a full-blown affair and ended up with him leaving his church, my mom, and our family. All because of porn. If you're reading this book and struggle with pornography, I want you to put it down and sign up for *xxxchurch.com*. Years ago, they saved my life from going down my father's exact path. I can't recommend this organization enough. They came and spoke at the college I went to, and I got to have lunch with one of their pastors. He gave me multiple suggestions on how to break the addiction and the curse, one of which was I had to tell the one person I didn't want to know. That was my fiancé and my now beautiful wife. I risked everything to tell her my biggest struggle in life. She loved me through it; today, we're stronger for it.

Every time we sin, we cover up our masterpiece little by little. Every white lie we tell, every time we are sexually impure in the eyes of God, or go against the two commandments Jesus gives us. These two commandments cover all ten that God gave to Moses. Love the Lord your God with all your heart, soul, and mind, and love your neighbor as yourself.

> *"Jesus replied, 'You must love the Lord your God with all your heart, all your soul, and all your mind.' This is the first and greatest commandment. A second is equally important: 'Love your neighbor as yourself.' The entire law and all the demands of the prophets are based on these two commandments.'" Matthew 20:37-40 NLT*

What does love your neighbor as yourself mean when your masterpiece is all covered with junk? Sometimes it's hard to love ourselves because of our sins and doubts. So how can we love our neighbor as ourselves when we don't even love ourselves? This book is about—finding your identity in Christ—learning to love yourself as He loves you.

FINDING YOUR MASTERPIECE

I know the title of this section isn't as fun as the last. It's just as important, though you may not like the results of what happens in this section. When I first did this, I had about ten pages worth of stuff I had to scrape off of my masterpiece. I had two pages the second time, and only five years had spanned the two moments. I couldn't believe how much stuff I had done in 5 years to others or myself that would cause me to have two pages worth of things I needed forgiveness for. So, what is this process I keep talking about? I call it taking stock of your life. In other words, you're scraping off all the junk you've piled onto your masterpiece over the years. Remember the illustration I used to reveal God's masterpiece to my church? That is precisely what you're going to be doing. You will take your metaphoric paint scraper and scrape off the junk on your masterpiece, just like I scraped off the shaving cream to reveal the masterpiece of a lion. Sometimes people can't see God's masterpiece until they realize that God loves them no matter what they bring to the table.

So how do we find our masterpiece? We start with taking stock of our lives. But how do we do that? In a minute, I'll have you bow your head and ask Holy Spirit some questions, and you'll listen for an answer. At the end of this chapter is a place for you to write down whatever Holy Spirit speaks to you. If you'd rather write it in a journal, please do that especially if you plan to share this book with others. You only get a page at the end of the chapter, so it may be wise to write it down in your journal. You can throw on some worship music or just sit in the quiet. But I need you to focus. This can become life-changing stuff for you. Taking stock of your life is about understanding the junk you've spread all over your masterpiece. We will discuss next how we get it off of us. Now you're going to ask Holy

> **WE COVER THAT MASTERPIECE WITH SIN, DOUBT AND FEAR, BUT UNDERNEATH IS STILL THE MASTERPIECE GOD CREATED.**

Spirit three questions:

Please reveal to me my wrongdoings to myself.
Please expose to me my wrongdoings to others.
Please show me how to make these things right.

The first is significant because we cannot move on to others
if we cannot forgive ourselves. The third one is essential
because sometimes we cannot make things right. After all,
someone may have died or moved on from our lives. But we
must forgive ourselves first in this process. Take a break from
reading this book and do the exercise. Even if you just get a
couple of things from Holy Spirit, it's a great start.

NOW WHAT?

Now that you have done that exercise and have the stock
of your life, the rest is easy. Just kidding, well, maybe, it all
depends on how much you want to be able to forgive. First,
tell someone about your wrongdoings. I know it may sound
crazy, but if you confess them to first yourself, then God,
and then to another person, you will be able to release them
and forgive much faster. The Bible tells us to do this in James
chapter 5. It also instructs us to pray for one another as we
do this.

> "Therefore, confess your sins to one another and pray for one
> another that you may be healed. The prayer of a righteous
> person has great power as it is working." James 5:16 ESV

What does this look like though? In a nutshell, you find a close friend who you trust. You then take them out to coffee or invite them over to your house if you want it to be more private. Then you just read them the list. You pray over each one that you read. It's as easy as that.

The next step is forgiving yourself or the person who did you wrong. It's easy to say I forgive someone, but it is sometimes challenging to ask for forgiveness. That's why you should ask for forgiveness from anyone you have done wrong. I had two people on my list that I had done wrong. One was a former best friend of mine that I had pushed away. The other was my mom. You see, I had a real struggle with betrayal. I was so afraid that everyone in my life would eventually leave that I subconsciously pushed them away. That's precisely what happened with my one friend. So I had to apologize to him and ask for his forgiveness. Luckily, I have since been freed of the fear of betrayal, and I no longer push the people closest to me away. Getting back to being friends was a rocky start, but we eventually got there. The hardest one was my mom. I had to admit to my mom that during my years as an alcoholic, I had lied to her about why I needed money for the electric bill, the house payment, or my car payment. I told her we were just short this month but didn't tell her why. Why I needed it was because I spent the money on booze. It was difficult to admit that to my mom and ask for forgiveness.

So, we've scraped off the junk on our masterpiece. What do we do next? That's a really great question. Next is that we live out our identity in Christ. We understand that we'll probably put more junk on, but we have the tools to scrape it off again. Understand that God calls you His masterpiece, and he created you as a masterpiece knowing that you would cover it up with junk.

WHY DO I MATTER?

YOU MATTER BECAUSE A MASTERPIECE IS STILL A MASTERPIECE EVEN WHEN IT'S COVERED UP.

You matter because a masterpiece is still a masterpiece even when it's covered up. We mentioned this in the beginning of the chapter. But I wanted to bring it up again because it is the reason you matter. You are a masterpiece, not just any masterpiece but God's masterpiece. He created you in his image and God doesn't make junk. So, you matter to God because he made you into His masterpiece. Even if you've covered it up with junk, sin, lies, or mud and dirt. a masterpiece is still a masterpiece even when it's covered up. You matter, I don't know how many times I'm going to say it throughout this book. But God made you into His masterpiece so you have to matter. Because why would he take that time to make you perfect if you didn't.

EXERCISE

After doing the exercise described in the previous chapter.
Discuss how you plan to heal.

_____

_____

_____

_____

_____

_____

_____

_____

_____

Imagination of Creation

*C*atchy title, right? I thought so. I call it this because there are so many imaginative aspects to us being created. We will look at them all, or at least some of them. Starting with one of my favorite verses in the Bible found in Isaiah, talking about how we are clay and God is the potter. The illustration of the potter's wheel is one that I love. The potter's wheel is difficult to work with without practice and yet so simple for God to form us out of clay. Have you ever made something with clay? It's not just the potter's wheel that's challenging to work with. It's also the clay. It has to be perfectly centered. It has to be perfectly wet to manipulate it. Too wet, and it won't hold up. Too dry, and it will crumble. However, in 5th-grade art class, I remember we used a potter's wheel to make mother's day gifts. It is funny that we are getting ready to celebrate my beautiful wife, mother, and mother-in-law this mother's day as I write this. However, it was so difficult trying to build a mug out of clay. I started over. I don't know how many times. But every time, I got better and better at it. I finally felt like a pro when it collapsed on me, and I had to start again. Eventually, I got something resembling a mug done and in the kiln to set. But knowing how difficult it is to manipulate clay makes Isaiah 64:8 means much more to me now than it did before learning how to work with clay.

"And yet, O Lord, You are our Father. We are the clay, and You are the potter. We all are formed by Your hand."
Isaiah 64:8 NLT

GOD'S ABILITY TO FORM US INTO WHO WE ARE FROM NOTHING BUT THE DUST OF THE EARTH IS PRETTY SPECTACULAR.

We are all formed by your hand. That phrase slaps (am I too old to say that?) Yes? Well, it's ok. We're past it now. What does it mean to be formed by the potter's hand? Unlike my mug-making ability, God's ability to form us into who we are from nothing but the dust of the earth is pretty spectacular.

FROM DUST, WE WERE MADE

That mother's day, I was so excited to give my mom her gift; it was something I formed with my hands. Something I made that was unique, and it was definitely one-of-a-kind. Just

like we are all unique and one-of-a-kind creations formed
by God's hands. God, the potter, created a masterpiece in
you; no two masterpieces are the same. Look at the mug I
made for my mom, no one in my class had a square mug
with a blue base and an orange handle. Some kids made
"ashtrays." Because they couldn't figure out how to get the
walls to stay standing. I, however, was determined to make it
work. I formed something from nothing like God did when
He created Adam. It says he formed man from dust, then
breathed life into him. Let's look at Genesis.

> *"Then the Lord God formed the man from the dust of*
> *the ground. He breathed the breath of life into the man's*
> *nostrils, and the man became a living person."*
> Genesis 2:7 *NLT*

Writing "breathed life" makes me think of the song Rattle
by Elevation Worship, which sidetracked me from where I
wanted to go with this. Let's go for the ride, shall we? When
God tells Ezekiel to prophesy to the bones. Prophesy to the
breath; the breath filled the dry bones as they came to life.
I sometimes wonder if when we feel spiritually dead, we
need to prophesy to the breath to fill our lungs, and it will
make us whole again. There was a time I felt spiritually dead
inside and couldn't figure out how to get out of it. I tried
everything. I would blast worship music. I would pray, and
nothing seemed to work. Then I started singing one of my
favorite worship songs which talks about breathing life into
my lungs. It's God's breath that we breathe daily, and it's
His breath that brings us life. "Great Are You, Lord", by All

Sons & Daughters saved my life. I somehow prophesied to the breath in my own life, and these dry bones came back to life.

Back to my train of thought, I probably should have mentioned I suffer from undiagnosed ADD. So, if things seem squirrelish (defined as, look, there's a squirrel), that's why. The Lord formed man out of dust. Can we just discuss how unbelievable that is for a moment? Out of dust. Out of stinking dust. What can we make with dust? We can make clay if you add water. Clay can make all sorts of things. Like my wife, you could create anything from clay if you're creative. Like me, you're limited to decorations, pots, mugs, and those little things you put in brown sugar to keep it from drying out. Did you have one of those? We did growing up. Dust is also one of those things in Wyoming that if you have hardwood floors, you're sweeping eight thousand times a day. Because it doesn't matter how often you've swept, you feel it if you take a step barefoot. The dust has crept into your house. That's all we can make from dust and our troubles with dust. God, on the other hand, made man. From dust! The most critical piece of this chapter is the creation aspect.

NEW CREATION

In the Bible, God calls us a new creation. This fits right in with our chapter and our book. One way to look at how to find our identity in Christ is to look at all He says about us. Why's that? Well, what He says about us helps us learn who we are in Him. So far in this book, we've learned that He calls us adopted, loved, friend and a masterpiece. So, let's recap this chapter. He formed us out of clay and made us from the dust of the earth. He breathed life into us. Those are some pretty incredible things! And now we're going to learn that He calls us a new creation.

"Therefore, if anyone is in Christ, the new creation has come: The old has gone, the new is here!" 2 Corinthians 5:17 NIV

If anyone has a relationship with Christ, they are a new creation. Their past is no longer there. It has been wiped from existence. You still remember it, and it has made you who you are today, but God is saying you no longer have to be that person because you are a new creation. You have been born again. Yes, the trials and tribulations you have endured have made this tough exterior that not even a knife could get through. Still, Jesus is telling you to strip off your tough exterior, get vulnerable with Him and allow Him to change you from the inside out. Because you are a new creation, those trials and tribulations are of the past, not your future. Is it scary? Yes! But we have a relationship with Jesus that will endure any fear we have. The song that always comes to mind when I'm talking about fear is the Veggie Tales song "God is Bigger Than the Boogieman" This song shaped my childhood when it comes to fear because if God is bigger than the Boogieman and the monsters on tv, then that's a pretty big God.

We can't allow fear to hold us back when it comes to accepting it when God calls us a new creation. I was fearful

WHY DO I MATTER?

when I first put my clay on the potter's wheel. For a moment, I thought maybe I'd fail, or it wouldn't be good enough for my mom. Our tongue and our mind have power.

> *"But no one can tame the tongue. It is restless and evil, full of deadly poison." James 3:8 NLT*

When we continually speak negativity over a situation, we will have a negative outcome ninety-nine percent of the time. That's not saying one hundred percent of the time; if you speak positively over a situation, it will always end with a positive outcome. Because sometimes, God shuts doors we're trying to open even when we speak positively. Don't worry. You're not alone.

JESUS IS TELLING YOU TO STRIP OFF YOUR TOUGH EXTERIOR, GET VULNERABLE WITH HIM AND ALLOW HIM TO CHANGE YOU FROM THE INSIDE OUT.

My wife gets on my case about speaking negatively over situations. I stop and think about the situation to remind myself to think positively. I let it marinate. If something seems a little off, I talk to my wife. I try not to gripe, complain, and mope around the house for days. Which we all do especially if the situation is out of our control. My wife got on my case the one time for being negative. I applied for a pastoral position. It was my first lead pastorate, and the head of the committee texted me at nine pm that night asking if we could talk the following day. I replied, of course, but I knew they had a meeting that morning with the whole committee, and it felt like some people were a little standoffish afterward. So I was already nervous about what they were discussing. So now that I get this text late at night, I'm on edge. I'm saying things like I'm not gonna sleep. They voted us out before I even got the chance to preach before them (rationally, I knew they didn't vote that morning). But I was on edge, to say the least. But I caught myself. My wife, and I prayed over the situation. It calmed me down and brought me to a place where I could accept any outcome from that call. It's just like the mug.

I could've said right at the gate, I can't make a mug. I'm not good enough. But I didn't. I sat down at the potter's wheel, trying my hardest. I must have restarted ten or twelve times. I finally got something resembling a mug. It took two class periods and a lot of hard work, but I got it made. If I had gone into it with the mindset most of us go into situations nowadays, I would have failed because I would have given up. We can't give up in the middle of the transformation process of becoming a new creation.

WHY DO I MATTER?

You matter because God created you. The story of me and the potter's wheel didn't end very well for the piece of clay I was sculpting. But my mom still loved it because I created it. God created you just like I created holy bowl and I loved it, I was so proud of it. And He loves you immensely too, He is so proud of you.

He never goes back on his love. He is not someone on earth

59

who will turn His back on you because you messed up. That's what religion teaches. What you have with God is a relationship. Religion says I need to hide from my father when I've done wrong. Relationship says I need my father when I mess up.

Which do you want? Honestly. Religion or Relationship. I know what I choose, I choose relationship ten times out of ten. Because there's no fear in the sense of being afraid. There is just love. That's why you matter!

<u>REFLECTION</u>

What does being a new creation in Christ mean to you?

_____

_____

_____

_____

_____

_____

_____

_____

_____

_____

CHAPTER SIX

Fearfully + Wonderfully Made

*P*salm 139 is a beautiful Psalm written by King David. It talks a lot about things we have already touched on, like how Ephesians mentions before God created the world, He chose you. Knowing what you would do in this life, He chose you. He knows your thoughts before you even think them, He knows what you'll do before you even do it, yet He chose you. There is nothing he doesn't know about us because he has already examined our hearts. And yet He chooses you. Because you are fearfully and wonderfully made.

He knows our coming and going; there is nowhere we can hide from Him. Yet sometimes we try. We shut the lights off to our mind hoping he doesn't see. But he knows every word we are going to speak before we speak it. The gossip, the slander, every word and yet He chose you. Because you are fearfully and wonderfully made.

IT IS NOT SOMETHING THAT WE EARN OR LOSE, BUT RATHER SOMETHING THAT IS INHERENT TO OUR IDENTITY AS CHILDREN OF GOD.

I knew this guy once who would always talk down on himself even though he was a great man of God. Even when people see us as great men of women of God though that doesn't mean our identities are rooted in Christ. He had no identity in Christ (and he knew it too), he was a stay at home dad (which I think is fantastic) and his identity was in keeping the house clean, getting the kids ready, making sure dinner was made and doing laundry all day. Then the 2020 pandemic hit and his life was flipped upside down. He didn't understand the concept that he was fearfully and wonderfully made by God. That he had to put his identity in Jesus. He had too many baskets holding his identity and in 2020-2022 he had to fill a new basket which was teacher for his kids. The baskets became too much to juggle for him. It almost seemed like he had given up on God. Like those years were so difficult that he began wondering if God truly existed. However, we can never escape God in anything that we do; we can try and run but he's pursuing us. There's nowhere we can hide from the Holy Spirit. We go to Heaven, He is there. We can go to the grave and He is there. If we go to the deepest oceans or the farthest desert, He is there. We cannot escape His presence. My friend eventually came back to the Lord it took a little bit and finding his identity in Christ to do it but he did and that's the most important thing. No more juggling baskets, he is still a stay at home dad, but that is not his identity. His identity is rooted in Christ. We are never too far from God to come back to Him. Just look what He says in Ezekiel.

> *"For this is what the Sovereign Lord says: I myself will search and find my sheep. I will be like a shepherd looking for his scattered flock. I will find my sheep and rescue them from all the places where they were scattered on that dark and cloudy day." Ezekiel 34:11-12 NLT*

> *"We love because he first loved us." 1 John 4:19 NIV*

He will pursue us. He's not the Kool-Aid man though. He's not going to come bursting through the walls of our heart to get to us. He's going to stand at the door and knock. He's a gentleman as a friend of mine put it. If we don't let Him in, he won't force his way in. He stands there and knocks. It's our job to open the door and let Him in.

THE BEAUTY IN THE BREAKDOWN

Being fearfully and wonderfully made is a phrase used in Psalm 139 to describe the intimate relationship between God and humanity. This phrase highlights the idea that each individual is unique and valuable, with a specific purpose and plan for their life. In the beauty and the breakdown, we will explore the concept of being fearfully and wonderfully made, its significance in Christian theology, and its practical implications for how we view ourselves and others.

The phrase "fearfully and wonderfully made" comes from
Psalm 139:14, which states.

> *"I praise you because I am fearfully and wonderfully*
> *made; your works are wonderful, I know that full well."*
> *Psalm 139:14 NIV*

This verse emphasizes the idea that each person is a work of
art, intricately designed and crafted by God. It acknowledges
that humans are not just another animal species but are
unique creations with a special place in God's plan.
The phrase "fearfully" in this context does not mean being
afraid or scared, but rather emphasizes the awe and reverence
that we should have for God's creation. It recognizes that our
bodies and souls are complex and intricate, with systems and
processes that we still do not fully understand. The phrase
"wonderfully made" emphasizes the idea that each person is
a marvel and a wonder, worthy of celebration
and admiration.

The concept of being fearfully and wonderfully made is
significant in Christian theology because it affirms the value
and dignity of every human being. It counters the idea that
humans are just another product of chance and evolution,
with no inherent value or purpose. Instead, it acknowledges
that each person is a unique and valuable creation of God,
with a specific plan and purpose for their life.

It is also important because it reminds us that our value and
worth do not depend on our achievements, appearance, or

status. It is not something that we earn or lose, but rather something that is inherent to our identity as children of God. This can be a powerful antidote to the pressures and insecurities of modern society, where we are bombarded with messages that tell us we are not good enough or that we need to constantly strive for more.

ASPECTS OF OUR BEING

The phrase "fearfully and wonderfully made" applies to every aspect of our being, from our physical bodies to our emotional and spiritual selves.

1. PHYSICAL BODY

The human body is a remarkable creation. It is designed to function in a specific way, with all the organs, tissues, and cells working together to keep us alive and healthy. Each person's body is unique, with different features and characteristics that make us who we are. Our bodies are capable of incredible things, like healing from injuries, adapting to new environments, and creating new life. When we think about how complex and intricate our bodies are, it is truly a wonder.

2. MIND

Our minds are equally remarkable. They are capable of processing vast amounts of information, solving complex problems, and creating new ideas. Each person's mind is unique, with different thought patterns and ways of processing information. Our minds can be trained and developed through learning, practice, and experience. When we think about how our minds work and how they shape our experiences of the world, it is truly a wonder.

3. SPIRIT

Our spirits are also part of being "fearfully and wonderfully made." Our spirits are what give us a sense of purpose, meaning, and connection to something greater than ourselves. They are the source of our deepest desires, fears, and hopes. Each person's spirit is unique, with different beliefs, values, and experiences shaping it. When we think about the depth and complexity of our spirit, it is truly a wonder.

WE CAN APPRECIATE THE BEAUTY AND DIVERSITY OF GOD'S CREATION...

SELF-IMAGE

The phrase "fearfully and wonderfully made" has important implications for how we view ourselves as human beings. It reminds us that we are not accidents or mistakes, but rather intentional creations of God, with inherent value and worth. This understanding is deeply comforting and empowering, especially in a world that often measures our worth by external factors such as appearance, wealth, or status.

Being fearfully and wonderfully made also has practical implications for how we view and treat ourselves and others. If we believe that each person is a unique and valuable creation of God, then we will be more likely to treat ourselves and others with respect, kindness, and compassion. We will be less likely to judge or compare ourselves to others, recognizing that our differences are part of what makes us valuable and special.

It can also help us to overcome prejudice and discrimination, as we recognize that each person is a unique and valuable creation of God, regardless of their race, ethnicity, gender, or other characteristics. We will be more likely to celebrate diversity and work towards justice and equality for all.

When we recognize that we are "fearfully and wonderfully" made, we can begin to see ourselves and others in a new light. We can appreciate the beauty and diversity of God's creation and celebrate the unique gifts and talents that each person brings to the world. We can also be more compassionate and understanding towards others, recognizing that they too are fearfully and wonderfully made, and deserving of love and respect.

At the same time, it is important to recognize that being fearfully and wonderfully made does not mean that we are perfect or immune to sin and brokenness. We are all flawed and imperfect, and in constant need of God's mercy and grace. However, recognizing our inherent value and worth as God's creations can help us to overcome feelings of shame, guilt, and inadequacy, and to embrace the fullness of life that God has for us.

Our self-image or self-worth bring us closer to God when we in fact look at ourselves as we should and that is as "fearfully and wonderfully made." As God's adopted child. As God's friend. Why do you matter? Because God says you do. Your self-image needs to be in Jesus. We mentioned earlier that our identity hinges on Jesus. Why you matter hinges on your self-image relying on Jesus.

WHY DO I MATTER?

EYES SO BEAUTIFUL AND SO UNIQUE IT'S WHERE PEOPLE GAZE WHEN THEY SPEAK TO YOU.

Let's answer this question for this chapter. You matter because God calls you fearfully and wonderfully made.

We broke down what each word means where fearfully is not afraid but in awe, and wonderfully is with such meticulous care. Psalms 139:14 states that His workmanship is marvelous, it's like nothing else. He calls you fearfully and wonderfully made because he created you from nothing.

He knit you together in your mother's womb. He breathed life into your lungs. He gave you a heartbeat like no one else's heartbeat. Fingerprints like no one else in the world. Eyes so beautiful and so unique it's where people gaze when they speak to you. You matter because of all of this. Because He calls you Fearfully and Wonderfully Made.

Being fearfully and wonderfully made is a powerful and affirming concept that emphasizes the unique value and dignity of every human being. It affirms our identity as beloved children of God, with a specific plan and purpose for our life. It has practical implications for how we view ourselves and others, leading us to treat each person with respect, kindness, and compassion. It can also help us to overcome prejudice and discrimination, celebrating diversity and working towards justice and equality for all. That's why you matter!

<u>REFLECTION</u>

How does knowing you are fearfully and wonderfully made, make you see yourself?

_____

_____

_____

_____

_____

_____

_____

_____

CHAPTER SEVEN

It's Christmas Time

I was in a band when I was younger, and the keyboardist and I broke off and tried to make our own EDM group. For those of you that don't know that means Electronic Dance Music. We wrote this song "It's Christmas Time" it had clips of Buddy the elf yelling I'm so excited and vocal effects of us singing it's Christmas time. It was an awesome song and I kind of wish I still had it today. All that to say Christmas is one of the best times of year not just because of the gifts but the ultimate gift we were given by God, His one and only son. The other gifts are pretty great too and if you didn't think, that you just lied and need to repent. But did you know that God calls us gifted? Not the I wrapped myself under the tree as the greatest gift of all gifted, but truly gifted. By the gifts and talents He gives us.

Some of you may have a hard time with this one especially.
Because identifying as gifted isn't easy when you don't
understand your gifting. But God calls you gifted. Not only
does he call you gifted, He has freely given each of us His
gifts and talents. Not everyone has the same gift or talents
just like not everyone has the same passions. Oscar Wilde said
"Be yourself, everyone else is already taken". Just like we read
earlier, we were created in Gods image uniquely and just like
that we have uniquely been given gifts, talents and passions to
be used for ministry and in our life.

> *"We have different gifts, according to the grace given
> to each of us." Romans 12:6a NIV*

NOT THE I WRAPPED MYSELF UNDER THE TREE AS THE GREATEST GIFT OF ALL GIFTED, BUT TRULY GIFTED.

God's gifting is His distinctive stamp
of value on each one of His children.
He gifts you talents and abilities to
use for His glory. He gives you the
ability to do the job He puts you in.
Never doubt, He equips the called
so if He has placed you in a role at
a certain job you have the gifts and
talents to do it because He has given
them to you. Ecclesiastes 5 says that it's a good thing to enjoy
the health and wealth God has given you. To enjoy the job,
He has placed you in to its fullest because it is indeed a gift
from God. And in Ecclesiastes 3 it states that people should
eat and drink of the fruits of their labor for these are gifts
from God. You are Gifted and Talented. I have a friend I
would say one of my closest friends who when I found these

two verses I texted immediately because he hates his job. But God placed him there. He placed him in the position he is in, gave him the money he needs to live and while he may hate his job, he is enjoying the fruits of his labor because it is a gift from God.

I have great friends. I'm very lucky. From the drum set in the living room to video messages that make me laugh uncontrollably, to heartfelt messages when I need them the most. To the gifts they buy me on my birthday and Christmas. Don't ever take your friends or your gifts for granted. Friends are a gift, and they are sent to you for 2 reasons. The first is for a season, you may only have these friends for a short time but they were there to help you through a trial, a blessing or even just a moment that you needed some encouragement. The second is life long friendships, these are friends that are in it for the long haul, through thick and thin. The point is no matter what you are gifted, whether its from the gifts and talents God has bestowed upon you or through your friendships you are gifted and that may make some people jealous. But that's on them not on you unless you use your gifts and talents to purposely make others jealous.

TOO TALENTED FOR JEALOUSY

I had a friend tell me I was too talented once. He said he was jealous of how many talents I had been blessed with. I'm not here to toot my own horn. But everything I do besides preaching revolves around numbers. And I'm very good with numbers. This person could only see the talents in front of him not the hours of practice and work that go into doing everything I can do. I told him his spiritual gifting and talents were unique to him, he has different ones than I do. While we are both communicators, he is great with his hands and can build and fix stuff better than I ever could. It is easy to watch others and say I wish I had what they have instead of looking inward to see what you have. The grass isn't always greener on the other side. We all have gifting and talents that God blesses us with. This specific friend has the gift of healing and has been known to give words of wisdom. We can't take credit for our gifting and talents. They are giving to us by God. If you become jealous of what God gave to others, you need to check your own heart because your identity may not be rooted in Christ.

We should be lifting others up with our gifts and talents, not boasting. Jealousy and boasting are heart issues. If we are purposely using our gifts and talents to make others jealous then we run the risk of no longer using them to glorify God but to glorify self. Glorifying self is dangerous not only because we would be making ourselves a god and the ten commandments say to have no other gods before the one and only true God. We run the risk of becoming self-righteous instead of allowing God to make us Holy and Righteous in his way.

TOO GIFTED TO WORRY

Too gifted to worry about anything *"For I have not been given a spirit of fear"* 2 Timothy 1:7a. We have to focus on our gifts not the gifts that others have. When we get caught up worrying about others' gifts we can open ourselves up to jealousy or trying to boast about our own gifts to make us seem better, when we're not. We are all equal. I said it before I'm good with numbers, my buddy is good with his hands. We can both communicate the word to others. He's a little more outgoing than I am but we're equals, we are both children of the most high. We are both called Adopted, Loved, a Friend, Created, a Masterpiece, Fearfully and Wonderfully Made, Gifted and Talented.

It's Christmas Time. Why? Because you are gifted. You're too gifted to worry about tomorrow. To worry about yesterday. To worry about everything you can't control. You're too gifted to worry. When we worry, we fear. And like I said about it, we have not been given that spirit. Fear and worry can paralyze us and prevent us from doing what God has called us to do. We may be afraid of failure, rejection, or the unknown. But God has not given us a spirit of fear. But we have been given the spirit of power. The power that God gives us is not a power that comes from ourselves. It is not a power that we can manufacture or create. It is a power that comes from God Himself. When we trust in God and rely on His strength, we can do all things through Him who gives us strength (Philippians 4:13). You are too gifted to worry about fear.

SAVED BY GRACE

Ephesians 2:8 says *"For by grace you have been saved through faith, and this is not your own doing; it is the gift of God."* You have been saved by grace literally in the Word of God. But not only have you been saved by grace it is considered a gift from God. He calls you gifted because he has freely given grace. Which highlights the importance of grace and faith in the process of salvation. Grace is a central concept in Christianity, and it refers to the unmerited favor and love that God shows to humanity.

It is through the grace of God that we are saved and reconciled to Him. This means that our salvation is not something that we can earn or achieve through our own efforts, but it is a gift from God. Therefore, you are gifted.

Ephesians 2:8 emphasizes the role of faith in salvation. Faith is the belief and trust that we have in God and His promises. It is through our faith in Jesus Christ that we are saved, and not through our own works or deeds. This means that our salvation is not dependent on our own abilities or accomplishments, but it is a result of our faith in God and His saving power. It reminds us that our salvation is a gift from God. This means that we do not deserve it, nor can we earn it. It is freely given to us by God, out of His love and mercy for us. This is a humbling and awe-inspiring truth that should fill us with gratitude and a desire to serve God and His purposes.

It is the unity of grace and faith through our own faith in God's grace that we are saved. We cannot have one without the other. Our faith in God's grace is what allows us to receive the gift of salvation and to live a life that is pleasing to God. To receive this free gift. Ephesians 2:8 is a powerful and inspiring verse that reminds us of the central message of Christianity. It highlights the importance of grace and faith in the process of salvation, and it reminds us that our salvation is a gift from God that we cannot earn or deserve. It is a message of hope and love that should inspire us to live a life of faith and gratitude towards God.

THE GREAT GIFTS

The great gifts are gifts from Holy Spirit. Like it states in 1 Corinthians chapter 12, a spiritual gift is given to each of us like we discussed earlier in this chapter. Our spiritual gift is unique to us to use within the power of Holy Spirit. It's never about us: when it becomes about us, we need to check ourselves before we wreck ourselves. Ok, I know that phrase may not be as funny or meaningful to you, but it is to me. I had this floor mate in college who used to walk up to people all the time and utter those words. You better check yourself before you wreck yourself. But I think it works in this case because making our gifting about ourselves, will wreck ourselves. Let's take a look at 1 Corinthians chapter 12.

> *"There are diversities of gifts, but the same Spirit. There are differences of ministries, but the same Lord. And there are diversities of activities, but it is the same God who works all in all. But the manifestation of the Spirit is given to each one for the profit of all: for to one is given the word of wisdom*

> *through the Spirit, to another the word of knowledge through*
> *the same Spirit, to another faith by the same Spirit, to another*
> *gifts of healings by the same Spirit, to another the working of*
> *miracles, to another prophecy, to another discerning of spirits,*
> *to another different kinds of tongues, to another the*
> *interpretation of tongues. But one and the same Spirit*
> *works all these things, distributing to each one individually*
> *as He wills." 1 Corinthians 12:4-11 NKJV*

WORDS OF WISDOM

A lot of people get Words of Knowledge and Words of
Wisdom confused and even believe that they are the same
thing. Words of Knowledge is a revelation of a specific fact
for the person(s) you are interacting with. We will discuss that
more in the next section. However, they do work in tandem
along with Discerning of Spirits. Words of Wisdom is simply
put the wisdom of God. I use this gift more than I care to
admit (not because I'm ashamed of the gift but for the reason
why I need it).

I am bi-vocational and a lot of times my boss will give me
a project and I struggle with how to complete it or even
get started. This may sound weird, but I'll pray for God to
give me the wisdom to do this, for guidance on how to get
started. Any time I'm stuck, it's a simple prayer, God give
me the wisdom to be able to do this. A Word of Wisdom will
help you apply the knowledge you may already have in a
particular situation. Meaning my training and experience will
get me through but sometimes I need that little nudge from

God to remember I know how to do it.

WORDS OF KNOWLEDGE

The Word of Knowledge is significant in the Christian faith because it helps believers understand God's will and purpose for their lives. It also allows them to discern truth from falsehood, particularly related to spiritual matters. The word of knowledge can also provide comfort and encouragement to those who are struggling or in need of guidance. Words of Knowledge can be when God gives you a word for someone else. Something usually only they would know. A lot of times He will do this before He does something miraculous. I have a friend who Holy Spirit works in the gift of healing through him. But one time we were together, and God told him a man in church needed prayer for his back. That was his Word of Knowledge. Then we prayed for this gentleman's back and he was healed. If it wasn't for the Word of Knowledge he never would have known to pray for this man unless the man told us his back was bothering him, but God intervened and told my friend.

The first time I experienced a Word of Knowledge I was 18 and I was a leader in our church's youth group. There was an altar call at the end of the service and I was praying for the students as they came up for prayer. One particular student, as I was saying a generic prayer that had to do with what the altar call was about, God spoke and said this student was having issues with his father. So I stopped praying immediately and asked him if he was having issues with his father. They confirmed what God told me and we prayed. I don't know if what we prayed did anything for the father, but I know it began to change the heart of the student because he said he felt a weight lifted off of him. I was obedient in my first encounter with a Word of Knowledge. It was so cool to be used by God.

FAITH

The gift of Faith is one of the most powerful and significant gifts. It is a gift that enables believers to trust God fully and completely, even in the most difficult and trying circumstances. Developing and using the gift of faith requires a deep relationship with God and a willingness to trust Him completely. People who desire to develop this gift should spend time in prayer, reading and meditating on God's Word, and seeking the guidance of the Holy Spirit. It is important to surround yourself with other people who can provide support and encouragement during difficult times.

The gift of Faith is the gift my wife walks in daily. It's one I hope to walk in daily. But this is her gift. She believes the Bible because of her faith. She walks in Words of Knowledge because of her faith and the gift she's been given. To me this is one of the most powerful gifts; it's the one we all long for. The gift that if you had, you wouldn't have questions. My wife doesn't ask questions she just believes because she knows it to be true. It is what the gift of faith is all about. The most powerful thing for me watching her walk in this gift is when we hit a financial rock or if were stuck in a hard place,she

82

never waivers, she never asks why God why. She just believes that heaven has our back and when we pray our prayers get answered. The one thing I love most about my wife is her faith in Jesus.

HEALING

Healing is such an awesome portrayal of God's love in someone's life. He loves them so much that he is willing to heal them. I remember when I was just filled with the baptism of the holy spirit my pastor had me pray for a women with cancer. At her next appointment that week she got a report that the tumor was gone! Y'all the tumor was gone! I was so excited for her that God showed his love to her in a miraculous way. Now I don't want to get into the miraculous too much because that gift is coming up. Whenever I think of healing, one, I think of Jesus but two, I think of Peter. I think of the statement Jesus made that we would do even greater things than He (John 14:12). I think of Peter because people were gathering in Acts chapter 5 verses 15-16 and bringing the sick so that the shadow of Peter would heal them, and it did.

Jesus meant what he said in John 14:12 and Peter was proof of that in Acts 5:15-16. I was recently reading a book by Ty Buckingham *The Holy Spirit Is Not A Bird* and in it he has a chapter that he calls Your First Miracle. He gives you practical steps in seeing a miracle happen. Even though I promised I wouldn't talk about miracles in this section here we go. I bring this up because one of the steps is test it out.

I'm so guilty of praying for someone and walking away thinking God didn't do anything but I never gave Him a chance. Testing it out gives God the chance to show up and show off.

MIRACLES

Now I discussed this a little in the last section, but miracles are exactly what's in the name, they're miraculous. Miracles arc all thought the Bible like when Paul had handkerchiefs and aprons touch his arms and they healed the sick and cast out evil sprits in Acts 19. Or when they threw the dead man on the bones of Elisha and the man came back to life in 2 Kings 13. The gravestone being rolled away from Jesus' grave was another miraculous act. We could go on and on with miracles from the Bible. Healing and Miracles walk hand in hand because healing is a miracle. Sometimes I look at the miracles in the Bible and am in awe of what God wants to do for his people.

PROPHECY

Prophecy is much like Words of Knowledge and Words of Wisdom, this is when God gives you a word. It is edifying and can be filtered through scripture. Prophecy is seen all throughout the Bible with most of them dealing with Jesus' coming and eventual death and resurrection. But those prophecies were fulfilled by Jesus. With the two followers on the road to Emmaus Jesus appeared to them but God shut their eyes so they didn't know it was him. The began talking about all the things going on in Jerusalem, and Jesus began to show them all the prophecies that were fulfilled by His death and resurrection. The gift of Prophecy is simply explained as Giving the message of God in that moment. It does not always refer to the future, but it can. Like I said it is simply a message from God.

DISCERNMENT

As I'm writing this, I have been wanting to get here. This is the gift I walk in daily. We find the gift of the Discernment or Discerning of Spirits is only mentioned once in the New Testament. The nature of the gift is not explained or defined. Consequently, there are different ways in which the gift is understood by believers. Some believe that this gift is for discerning Prophecies, Words of Wisdom or Words of Knowledge, and also Interpretation of Tongues. There is another camp that believes it is to discern the character of a person. One more camp believes it is the discernment between Holy Spirit and Evil Spirits. There is also a camp the believes it is for all three. Simply put, it is to know something that you normally wouldn't know except through the power of Holy Spirit.

If you think about it, you wouldn't have uneasy feelings about a persons character unless Holy Spirit brought it up to you. You wouldn't be able to discern an evil spirit unless Holy Spirit brought it to your attention. And you wouldn't know if a Prophecy, or a Word of Knowledge or Word of Wisdom, or an Interpretation of Tongues was wrong unless Holy Spirit opened your heart and mind to it. So, I believe even though we don't have a clear definition of what it looks like, we can safely say it is knowing something you normally wouldn't know through the power of Holy Spirit.

TONGUES

The gift of Tongues is a special one. It is a gift for all people. Young and Old. On the Day of Pentecost the Holy Spirit fell upon the assembled believers and *"all of them were filled with the Holy Spirit and began to speak in other tongues"* (Acts 2:4). Later, as Peter was preaching at the house of Cornelius, *"the Holy Spirit came on all who heard the message"* and they were *"speaking in tongues and praising God"* (Acts 10:44, 46). Again, as the apostle Paul was ministering to the Ephesian disciples, *"the Holy Spirit came on them, and they spoke in tongues and prophesied"* (Acts 19:6). It is evident also that Paul himself was filled with the Holy Spirit (Acts 9:17) and spoke in tongues (1 Corinthians 14:18). This is what we call the IPE or Initial Physical Evidence of being Baptized in Holy Spirit.

It has two purposes. The first is as a prayer language, this is where you are in your prayer closet or while praying over someone and you don't know what to say, you can pray in your prayer language and you know what you are praying is coming from heaven. Praying in your prayer language is a special thing. I recently learned from Scott Wilson's book *Clear the Stage* that we can ask God to interpret our prayer language for us. It's changed my prayer life immensely, when I ask God to interpret my prayer language for me.

Sometimes, I'll get a word other times a phrase or a scripture verse. But it is always edifying, and it always makes me feel a little bit better.

The second purpose for speaking in tongues is a public utterance. In a Bible study or church service a person will publicly speak in tongues in a loud enough volume for everyone to hear. This should only happen if there is an interpretation to follow. And that's where we transition to our next spiritual gift.

WE SHOULD BE LIFTING OTHERS UP WITH OUR GIFTS AND TALENTS, NOT BOASTING.

INTERPRETATION OF TONGUES

This is going to be a short one since we basically covered it in the last section. When a public utterance of tongues takes place there should be an interpretation. That interpretation should be edifying and scriptural. *IF* at any moment it doesn't meet those two criteria it should be shut down.

SO WHICH SPIRITUAL GIFT DO I HAVE

I always say this, if one of these jumps off the page at you, it's probably the one you walk in. If not, just pray about it and ask God to reveal it to you!

WHY DO I MATTER

This is a long chapter and I don't want to make it even longer
for you. But we end every chapter with why do I matter?
So let's figure that out. God calls you gifted and not only
that, He provides the gifts and talents that He calls you.
For Freeeeeeee. Ok, have you ever seen the movie Bedtime
Stories with Adam Sandler. He's standing in front of the
sports car dealership and he's asking the guy For Freeeeeeeee?
That's what God does for your gifts and talents they are
freely given by Him for you to use throughout your life to
glorify Him.

REFLECTION

What does being called gifted mean to you?

_____

_____

_____

_____

_____

_____

_____

_____

_____

CHAPTER EIGHT

Grilled Ham + Cheese

I love, love, love a good grilled ham and cheese. I could probably eat one every day. But this chapter isn't about grilled ham and cheese per se. But it really is at the same time. Where am I going with this? Why don't you just come along for the ride? Let's take a look at some Scripture to help guide us in the right direction. No I don't think Paul had a grilled cheese in mind when he wrote this but my mind went there, so here we are.

> *"Now if we are children, then we are heirs—heirs of God and co-heirs with Christ, if indeed we share in his sufferings in order that we may also share in his glory."*
> *Romans 8:17 NIV*

For some background, Paul had just told the Romans that they are adopted children of God. That's funny we talked about that in the first chapter using a verse in Galatians. So, the reason Paul uses the analogy here of God adopting us as His children is because of the Roman adoption process. It was long and tedious a lot like our process today but a little worse. You see most adoptions were done so a father had an heir. So a family with nothing would put their son up for adoption and a wealthy family with no sons would adopt them. This is my version of the process so Its way more simplified than someone else's. Once the father has adopted the son, he must sell him back to his original father 3 times. This is where things get crazy. Then they must go before a board of elders from all different ages to witness the adoption. The reason is so when the father dies there is someone to say no, I witnessed that adoption if anyone tries to challenge that the heir is not really the heir. This part gets really good because in Romans 8:16 it states that Holy Spirit is the witness to our adoption. We don't need a board of elders; we don't need all different ages. All we need is Holy Spirit so when someone tries to deny that you or I are in fact a child of God, Holy Spirit can step up and say I witnessed the adoption. they are heirs to the kingdom.

INHERITANCE

So why grilled ham and cheese for a chapter talking about God calling you heir? Well my parents are from the camp that Jesus was/is going to come back in their lifetime. Well my dad passed in 2010 so that didn't happen. He wasn't even around for the 2012 End of Earth day parties we threw. Don't worry I'm at the point with my therapist where I can joke about my father's death now. But seriously he had no 401k, no life insurance, nothing, so I inherited nothing from him. He did make a bunch of cinnamon rolls for us? Yes, the kind that are all sticky and gooey. But nothing else. My mom is a little better, she has all the things and a few things for us kids to inherit. But it's not like she's a secret millionaire…are you?

Inheritance is a funny thing because you have people who get millions, people who get thousands or hundreds of thousands. Some people get priceless family heirlooms. Some people get nothing or possibly life-changing moments. Not me, we lost all of our family heirlooms in a flood and

> WE ARE CHILDREN OF GOD AND CHILDREN INHERIT, THAT'S JUST THEIR RIGHT.

then whatever survived the flood was lost in a fire. I don't know how much my mom plans on leaving us, but I do know she's at least as prepared as she can be. Building generational wealth is something most people can't do. But we can surely try. So why grilled cheese and ham sandwiches. As delicious as they are sometimes we feel like it's all we will inherit. It's a poverty mindset. Because inheritance is so much more than monetary value.

Growing up I ate more grilled ham and cheese sandwiches than I care to admit. Dinner, lunch, all the meals, grilled ham and cheese. And when I begin to think all I'm going to inherit is a grilled cheese and ham sandwich, I couldn't be more wrong. My mom worked hard to have what she has, and my wife and I do the same. We should honestly be grateful for what we inherit from anyone. I'm still holding out for that long lost rich aunt or uncle who listed me as the beneficiary of their estate. No? That's impossible? Maybe, but one can dream. I know something we inherit though. This heir is an heir to the Father that owns cattle on a thousand hills. A Kingdom fit for a king. Fit for me and you.

HEIR TO THE KINGDOM

Romans 8:17 talks about becoming heirs to God and His kingdom. Because we have been adopted, because we are children of God and children inherit that's just their right. Because we are Gods children we have full rights to receive His inheritance. We are His beneficiaries and Holy Spirit is our witness. Think about all that means, everything God has belongs to us as well, because we belong to Him. Our eternal inheritance as co-heirs with Christ is the result of the amazing grace of God. Peter writes in 1 Peter, that our inheritance can never spoil, never perish or fade.

> *"Praise be to the God and Father of our Lord Jesus Christ! In his great mercy he has given us new birth into a living hope through the resurrection of Jesus Christ from the dead, and into an inheritance that can never perish, spoil or fade. This inheritance is kept in heaven for you, who through faith are shielded by God's power until the coming of the salvation that*

is ready to be revealed in the last time." 1 Peter 1:3-5 NIV

When we talk about inheriting the kingdom there's a group of people that come to mind and that is the Israelites. They inherited the promise land. The twelve spies tasted the grapes and the honey. But yet ten out of twelve decided the giants were too big and the armies too strong for God to handle. It was their inheritance. It was theirs for the taking but they let fear get in their way. Fear isn't of God. It's not a trait of God, yes we are called to fear God but in a humbling reverent way. Fear is a liar as the song goes. Or my new favorite phrase is "it's stage 4 licabities." All joking aside, fear can be crippling. For the Israelites it was just that, so crippling they would rather go backwards than move forward into their promise, into their inheritance. How would you feel if in your job you just kept going down the ladder instead of up it to new heights? It wouldn't feel very good, would it? That's exactly what its like when we don't step into our inheritance. It's like taking one step forward and two steps back. Or climbing down a ladder when we should be climbing up. Speaking of climbing ladders I had never seen someone run down a ladder until the other day. We were hanging something, and my buddy runs down a ladder like he was running down steps it was crazy but it reminded me of going backwards. As I was working on this chapter it reminded me that when we go backwards, we walk right out of our inheritance just like the Israelites did. But the beauty of God is He's not a one and done God. In Joshua we read that the Israelites do in fact make it into the promise land in crazy God like fashion. In Hebrews we learn we need to persevere so we get what He promised. Check out the actual verse.

> *"You need to persevere so that when you have done the will of God, you will receive what he has promised."*
> Hebrews 10:36 NIV

DON'T STOP AT SIX, SEVEN'S ON ITS WAY

The Israelites marched around Jericho for six days with nothing happening. But God had a plan. March around the walls once a day for 6 days and on the seventh day march around seven times and then give a loud shout. But the people and the armies were just following Joshua. They didn't know the plan. They just marched for 6 days. Came home and rested. Could you imagine being one of the warriors going home to his wife. She's all asking him how war was and all he has to say is we marched around Jericho quietly one time and came home...It would have been easy for them to give up on the sixth day. Well, I guess we're not getting our inheritance. Nothing's happening. Not even a brick fell in all of our quiet marching. But they didn't, they kept following Joshua's orders . They kept marching and on the seventh day at the seventh time, Joshua yelled shout and the walls came a tumbling down. Don't stop at six, don't stop when it looks bleak. When nothing's going your way. When everything around you is failing and you don't know why. Don't stop when you're at six because seven is on its way. The day of reckoning is on its way. The day of your inheritance is on its way. Seven is on its way and it's coming at you like a freight train. It's not gonna stop for anything but it's coming to take you to a place you've never been. It's coming to take you to new heights you've never seen. I did a wedding once on the summit of a mountain. About ten thousand feet above sea level. I was standing at a new height that I had never been to. Before this wedding the highest I had ever been was seven thousand feet. It is one of the most beautiful places I have ever seen. You feel like you're in the clouds. You can truly see God's master craftsmanship at work when you are standing that high. I was brought to a new height physically so I could see new things and do new things. God wants to do that for you spiritually.

THE FRUIT OF INHERITANCE

Matthew 5:5 states *"Blessed are the gentle, for they shall inherit the earth."* Your fruit matters. Gentleness is one of the fruits of the spirit and in order to inherit the earth Matthew writes we must be gentle. Growing fruit is an ugly job. It belongs on Mike Rowe's Dirty Jobs. Why is that, because in order to grow fruit you need to do things that to the world aren't the most beautiful. Like fasting, we are called to fast and pray. I like cheeseburgers, I like french fries. Take that away from me for 21 days and we are throwing hands. It's not pretty. Things that are fruitful take ugly work. You ever pray so hard, you ugly cry? Read Gods word and the tears start rolling, mascara running everywhere, it doesn't matter if it's waterproof. We need to be fruitful. We need to bear fruit, for you will know them by their fruit.

"Beware of false prophets, who come to you in sheep's clothing but inwardly are ravenous wolves. You will recognize them by their fruits. Are grapes gathered from thornbushes, or figs from thistles? So, every healthy tree bears good fruit, but the diseased tree bears bad fruit. A healthy tree cannot bear bad fruit, nor can a diseased tree bear good fruit. Every tree that does not bear good fruit is cut down and thrown into the fire. Thus you will recognize them by their fruits." Matthew 7:15-20 ESV

THE DAY OF YOUR INHERITANCE IS ON ITS WAY.

What does good fruit look like? Well, we get a pretty good idea from Paul in Galatians where he lists the fruits of the Spirit. These are important because if we are rooted in God's word, spend time with Him every day and live a life of worship and devotion to Him we will bear good fruit. But none of those things are pretty. They take hard work and dedication. Because of our nature, even though God has chosen us and has an inheritance waiting for us, we must work through our sinful nature to produce good fruit. What are those fruits? I'm glad you asked.

"But the fruit of the Spirit is love, joy, peace, forbearance, kindness, goodness, faithfulness, gentleness and self-control. Against such things there is no law." Galatians 5:22-23

We inherit these fruits when we have a full-on relationship with God. Like I stated earlier, we must be rooted in God's

Word, spending time with Him daily and live a lifestyle
of worship to the King. See worship isn't just for Sunday
mornings and it's not just singing songs we like to sing.
It's not just about raising your hands in surrender. It's
about all of that, spending time with God and in His Word
included. But it's a lifestyle, it's walking in an identity, it's
walking in good fruit, but more importantly it's walking in
your inheritance.

WHY DO I MATTER?

You matter because God calls you heir. It means that even
if you don't have an earthly inheritance, even if you're
only inheriting a grilled ham and cheese or a cinnamon roll
recipe., you have a heavenly inheritance fit for a king. Fit for
you and me. We're not perfect, sometimes we grow bad fruit.
But the grace of God is sufficient for all of us. God calls you
Adopted, Loved, Friend, Masterpiece, Created, Fearfully
and Wonderfully Made, Gifted and Talented, and Heir. You
matter because God calls you heir.

REFLECTION

What are you set to inherit? On this earth or spiritually?
Which is more important to you and why?

_____

_____

_____

_____

_____

_____

_____

_____

CHAPTER NINE

Deserve Nothing, Gain Everything

*I*magine this: God sees us as forgiven, no strings attached. His grace is like a steady anchor for our souls, even in those quiet moments where we tend to replay our mistakes. Deep down, there's this sacred invitation from God, reaching beyond our flaws. It's an invitation to embrace forgiveness, to bask in a love that goes way beyond what we can grasp, and to walk in the warm glow of God's mercy.

This chapter dives into the amazing idea that God sees us as forgiven, a truth that really hits home and speaks to the very core of who we are. It's not about deserving it or earning grace – we just get it freely. So, think of it like deserving nothing but gaining everything. Forgiveness can be a tough concept for us to wrap our heads around because, in our culture, it's hard to believe in something that's given freely.

I remember struggling a lot with asking for forgiveness, especially for my anger issues. It became a routine until one day, I heard this small, calming voice saying, My child, I've already forgiven you for that. That moment led me to 2 Chronicles 7:14:

> *"If my people, who are called by my name, will humble themselves and pray and seek my face and turn from their wicked ways, I will hear from heaven and will forgive their sins and restore their land." 2 Chronicles 7:14 NLT*

GOD'S CALL ISN'T THIS LOUD JUDGMENT; IT'S MORE LIKE A GENTLE WHISPER THAT SEEPS INTO OUR THOUGHTS.

Picture a moment of stillness, where the weight of your mistakes meets the soothing whispers of forgiveness. In those sacred spaces, God invites you to let go of guilt and step into the freedom of redemption. When God calls us forgiven, it's not about pointing fingers; it's a melody of compassion echoing through the chambers of our hearts. Life is like this intricate tapestry, right? Each thread of our mistakes gets met with God's forgiving needle. It's like this weaving process that patches up the fabric of our existence, turning our stains into a masterpiece of grace. God's call isn't this loud judgment; it's more like a gentle whisper that seeps into our thoughts, assuring us that our sins, no matter how deep, can be washed away, made as white as snow. Cool, huh?

THE PARADOX OF UNEARNED FORGIVENESS

Let's talk forgiveness for a sec! So, in our way of thinking, forgiveness usually comes with a side of remorse and a promise to do better—a bit of a transaction, you know? But here's the twist in God's playbook: being forgiven is way beyond this human give-and-take. It's this mind-bending truth that flips our understanding on its head because, in God's language, forgiveness is handed out for free, no strings attached, not earned or deserved.

God doesn't dangle forgiveness like a carrot for being good. Nope, it's more like a response to our brokenness, a steady stream of divine love that keeps flowing, no matter how hard or not we try. So, when God says we're forgiven, it's an invite to grab onto this unearned grace, drop the self-defense, and soak up the glow of a love that doesn't care about conditions. It's not just a label; it's like stepping into the warm hug of divine mercy. Imagine a beat-up soul, weathered by life's storms, finding comfort in the arms of a caring Creator. In God's world, mercy isn't a far-off idea but a real force that heals the heart and breathes life into the weary spirit.

Ever heard that saying from Matthew 5:7? *"Blessed are the merciful, for they will be shown mercy."* It's a nugget of wisdom, right? In our daily dealings, mercy tends to be a bit scarce, saved for those who've earned it or said sorry. But in God's system, mercy flows generously to the repentant and the wanderers alike. It's like this river of compassion that wipes away the mess of sin and shame, leaving behind a landscape decorated with forgiveness.

Check out Psalms 145:8 too:

> *"The Lord is gracious and compassionate, slow to anger and rich in love."*

That's the atmosphere we're talking about—a God who's all about grace and love, not quick to get mad. It's like a breath of fresh air in a world where forgiveness can sometimes feel like a rare flower.

THE JOURNEY OF FORGIVENESS

How do we respond when God calls us forgiven? The answer lies in the life-changing power of acceptance. Acceptance of our imperfections, acknowledgment of our need for forgiveness, and the willingness to let go of the chains that bind us to our past mistakes. God's call to forgiveness is an invitation to a sacred dance of surrender and acceptance, where our brokenness meets the mending touch of God's love.

In the symphony of redemption, our response is a harmonious melody that echoes through the corridors of eternity. It is a resounding 'yes' to God's offer of forgiveness, a surrender of our pride and self-sufficiency at the feet of God's grace. As we accept the truth of being forgiven, we step into a new reality, a reality where the burdens of guilt are replaced by the wings of freedom, and the shadows of shame are dispelled by the light of God's acceptance.

Being called forgiven is not the end but the beginning of a life-changing journey. It is an initiation into a process of renewal, where the old self, burdened by sin, is crucified, and a new self, clothed in righteousness, emerges. This journey is not always easy, for the path of transformation requires courage and vulnerability. Yet, it is a journey accompanied by God's presence, a journey where the footsteps of grace guide us through the wilderness of change.

In the language of the soul, transformation is a gradual unfolding, a metamorphosis from the caterpillar of sin to the butterfly of righteousness. It is a process where the scars of the past become testimonies of God's redeeming power, and the broken pieces of our lives are fashioned into a mosaic of divine beauty. Being called forgiven by God sets the tone for who we are in Christ. It sets the tone of our identity in Him and surpasses all understanding of what we could ever imagine it to be. Forgiveness in a Godly sense is never wavering, it's completely steady, it never ebbs and flows; we are called to forgive others as we have been forgiven. Just as loving others as ourselves means we must love ourselves before we can love others. We must also forgive ourselves as we forgive others. In 12 step recovery programs you learn the hardest person to forgive is yourself. Once that happens, forgiving others is like a walk in the park. Not really but we can hope for things not yet seen. As we bask in the warmth of

God's forgiveness, we are called not only to receive but also to extend this grace to others. The language of God calling us forgiven becomes a language of compassion, spoken through our actions and attitudes. In a world marred by judgment and condemnation, our lives become a living testament to the life-changing power of God's love.

FORGIVENESS IN A GODLY SENSE IS NEVER WAVERING, IT'S COMPLETELY STEADY, IT NEVER EBBS AND FLOWS.

Extending forgiveness to others is not a duty but a privilege, an opportunity to be co-creators of a world bathed in the hues of forgiveness. It is a call to emulate God's language of grace in our relationships, to forgive as we have been forgiven, and to be bearers of the light that dispels the darkness of unforgiveness.

SAVED BY HIS GRACE

"God saved you by His grace when you believed.
And you can't take credit for this; it is a gift from God."
Ephesians 2:8 NLT

Imagine forgiveness as a grand masterpiece painted on the canvas of grace. Ephesians 2:8 whispers to us in the quiet moments, reminding us that forgiveness isn't earned through an exhaustive checklist of good deeds. It's not a trophy for the most virtuous or the least flawed. No, it's a symphony of grace playing in the background of our lives, an exquisite melody that sways with the rhythm of our belief.

"God saved you by his grace." Let that truth envelop you. It's not a distant, indifferent salvation. It's a saving grace that pulls you close, like a comforting embrace in your darkest moments. It's the kind of grace that reaches down into the messiness of our lives and says, I've got you.

"But when you believed." Picture this: your belief is like a flare in the night sky, signaling to God that you trust His grace, that you're willing to surrender your brokenness. It's not about having it all together; it's about taking that leap of faith and believing that there's a love beyond comprehension waiting to catch you.

"And you can't take credit for this." In a world obsessed with accolades and recognition, this line hits like a gentle reminder. You can't boast about earning forgiveness; it's not a badge of honor you display. It's a humbling acknowledgment that the credit belongs to the One who freely gives, not to the one who strives to earn.

It is a gift from God. Here's the emotional core of forgiveness. Imagine a beautifully wrapped gift, not because you deserve it, but simply because you are cherished. This gift of forgiveness is an outpouring of divine love, a love that says, I know your flaws, your stumbles, and I choose to forgive because you are worth it.

In the realm of forgiveness, Ephesians 2:8 is an invitation to release the heavy burdens of guilt and shame. It's God extending His hand, saying, "I've forgiven you, now let go."

Forgiveness isn't a transaction; it's a gift exchange. You offer your brokenness, and God gives you grace, forgiveness, and a chance at a new beginning.

So, let this verse be a lighthouse in the storm of guilt, guiding you to the shores of forgiveness. It's not about deserving, earning, or striving. It's about accepting the gift of grace, letting it flood your soul, and embracing the freedom it brings. Ephesians 2:8 is an emotional anthem of forgiveness, echoing through the chambers of your heart, reminding you that you are forgiven, loved, and free.

WHY DO I MATTER

In the place where God calls us forgiven, we encounter a love that transcends our understanding, a love that speaks to the depths of our being in a language of grace and redemption. It is a call to release the shackles of guilt, to embrace the paradox of unearned forgiveness, and to walk the life-changing journey of renewal.

As we respond to God's call, our lives become a symphony of acceptance and surrender, a harmonious melody that echoes through the corridors of eternity. The journey of transformation unfolds, guided by the healing power of divine mercy, and we find ourselves not only recipients but also conduits of God's grace that beckons all to be forgiven.

May we, as bearers of God's forgiveness, extend it to others and yourself, creating a tapestry of forgiveness that covers the world in the warmth of God's unending love.

So, why do you matter? Because God calls you forgiven, and He calls you to forgive not just others but yourself. God loves you so much He sent his son so that you could be shown grace and mercy for your sins. So that He could freely call you forgiven.

REFLECTION

When God calls you Forgiven He does it freely. How do we offer the same forgiveness to others?

_____

_____

_____

_____

_____

_____

_____

_____

CHAPTER TEN

Free Falling

ecause I'm free, free falling. Did you sing it? I did when I wrote it and about a thousand times after that. It just got stuck in my head. God calls us free, free from fear, free from slavery, free from our addictions and afflictions and so much more. But we are free! To be truly free you must be submissive to the Father. What does that mean? Take a wild horse for example, they run free. But for a horse to be used to its purpose the cowboy must break them, so they can ride them. Horses have many purposes in life, they have many talents just like we do and in a lot of ways their emotions and mental state are a lot like that of humans. You're not here for a lesson on horses though so let's get to the point. A rider must break the horse; it must become submissive to its master. So that way if they are out in the wild wrangling cattle it will do what its master commands it to do. A horse or us may plan our way but only the father directs our steps.

> *"The heart of man plans his way, but the Lord establishes his steps."* Proverbs 16:9 ESV

He will lead us to food and water much like the rider leads the horse. Look what he did for the Israelites in the wilderness. He provided mana and water every day. In your wilderness you will have everything you need to survive because God establishes our steps. He provides a way when there seems to be no way. They were eventually set free from the wilderness and entered their inheritance like we discussed in the Grilled Ham and Cheese chapter. They were freed from slavery in Egypt and freed from their own punishment in the wilderness. There are so many examples of freedom in the Bible. Whether it's freedom from sins or physical ailments. Jesus was there for it all.

IN YOUR WILDERNESS YOU WILL HAVE EVERYTHING YOU NEED TO SURVIVE

> *"Now the Lord is the Spirit, and where the Spirit of the Lord is, there is freedom."* 2 Corinthians 3:17 NIV

The concept of freedom is deeply ingrained in us. We long for freedom in various aspects of our lives, freedom from oppression, freedom from fear, and freedom from our sin. In reading the following verse, we will see the beautiful truth that God calls us to, a profound and liberating freedom.

> *"You, my brothers and sisters, were called to be free. But do*
> *not use your freedom to indulge the flesh; rather, serve one*
> *another humbly in love. For the entire law is fulfilled*
> *in keeping this one command: 'Love your neighbor as yourself.'"*
> Galatians 5:13-14 NIV

In Galatians 5, the Apostle Paul declares that we were
called to be free. This is not a call to a temporary escape
or a fleeting moment of liberty, but a profound call to live
in a state of freedom, rooted in our identity as children of
God. God's desire is for us to experience a freedom that goes
beyond circumstances, a freedom that is found in Christ
alone. While God calls us free, He also instructs us on how
to use that freedom responsibly. We are not to use our liberty
as an excuse for self-indulgence or as a license to engage in
sinful behavior. Instead, God calls us to a different kind of
freedom, a freedom that is expressed through selfless service
and humble love. Our liberty in Christ is not a call to live for
ourselves but an opportunity to love and serve one another.

> *"So if the Son sets you free, you will be free indeed."*
> John 8:36 NIV

You have been set free by the death and resurrection of our
Lord and Savior. How amazing is that? Freedom from sin,
from death, from life without a connection to our Heavenly
Father. We have been not only called free but we have been
set free. Before Jesus' death and resurrection, we basically
had our fingers in a Chinese finger trap and couldn't get out.

CHINESE FINGER TRAP

Remember those things? I would always get one in my stocking at Christmas time for some reason and I loved playing with them. But your fingers got stuck and in order to get them free you had to push in and pull at the same time. Jesus' death and resurrection is a lot like the push and pull of the Chinese finger trap, He set us free. Because we have been set free God now calls us free. The essence of God's call to freedom is beautifully encapsulated in the command to "love your neighbor as yourself." In loving others, we fulfill the entire law. True freedom, according to God's design, is intimately connected with love. It is a freedom that liberates us from the bondage of selfishness and empowers us to live in love, reflecting the character of our Heavenly Father. Much like the bondage of a Chinese finger trap the love Jesus has for us has set us free and I can't say it enough, He calls us free because we've been set free.

God's freedom is so we can finally break the chains that bind us. Chains of sin, guilt, fear, and societal expectations. Through Christ's redeeming work, we are set free from the power of sin, and we are invited to walk in the light of God's grace. As we accept this call to freedom, we become superheroes, sharing the message of hope with those still entangled in the bondage of sin. I have a friend who once posted on Facebook if you knew me in my addiction you have to know by now that Jesus is real. What a redemption story. If you knew me at my worst and see me now, how could you not know Jesus is real?

YOU WERE CREATED FOR IT

From the very beginning, God created us with the gift of freedom. In the Garden of Eden, Adam and Eve had the freedom to choose. God did not create robots programmed to obey; instead, He gave us the dignity of free will. Our freedom is an essential part of being made in the image of God. One significant reason God calls us free is the liberation from the bondage of sin. Sin entangles and enslaves, but through Christ, we find the ultimate liberation. The sacrifice of Jesus on the cross broke the chains of sin, offering us forgiveness and a new life. God's call to freedom is an invitation to leave the old life behind and walk in the freedom that only Christ can provide.

God desires a genuine and loving relationship with His children. True love cannot be coerced; it must be freely given. God's call to freedom is an invitation to choose Him willingly, to love Him with hearts that have the freedom to respond. In this freedom, we discover the depth of His grace and the beauty of a relationship that is founded on love, not coercion. God's call to freedom is also a call to purposeful living. When we embrace the freedom found in Christ, we discover our true identity and purpose. We are set free to live a life that reflects the character of God, to love and serve others, and to fulfill the unique calling He has placed on each of our lives. Freedom in Christ is not license for aimless living but an empowerment for purposeful living which we discussed in a section above. We have to understand that we are free for so many reasons other than what our minds can imagine.

In a world marred by brokenness and oppression, God's call to freedom becomes a beacon of hope. It is a declaration that no matter how entangled we may be in the struggles of life, there is a way to freedom through Jesus Christ. God's call echoes through the ages, inviting all to experience the true freedom that comes from knowing and following Him. Our freedom is not to be taken lightly, but rather cherished as an invitation to live in love, purpose, and relationship with our Creator. We've talked a lot about love in this book. I think it stems from that being the central theme of the Bible and God being a God of love. Freedom in itself is an act of love. So being that the creator of the galaxies calls you free, that's pretty special.

WHY DO I MATTER?

JESUS' DEATH AND RESURRECTION IS A LOT LIKE THE PUSH AND PULL OF THE CHINESE FINGER TRAP, HE SET US FREE.

You matter because you were created in the image of God which automatically makes you free. More importantly God calls you free, and he gave us free will. It was in God's will for Adam and Eve to walk and talk with Him, that's why the garden was so special. Our hearts are like a spiritual Garden of Eden, where Holy Spirit walks with you in the cool of the day, bringing joy, peace, fellowship, warmth, comfort, and fulfillment in your life. Building a place for Holy Spirit to dwell is like restoring the paradise of Eden in your life. The garden was special but sin entered the world, so God had to send His Son to die on the cross and to rise again three days later so that we could finally be free once again and so that the relationship between humanity and God could once again exist. So, why do you matter? Because God restored the garden inside of you so you could be free and walk alongside of Him, spending time with Him and learning about Him. He did all that for you! He will do so much more too.

REFLECTION

What does it mean to you to be truly free?

_____

_____

_____

_____

_____

_____

_____

_____

CHAPTER ELEVEN

Rescued, Not Abandoned

God calls us us redeemed, which means we are rescued and not abandoned. We are restored. We are recovered. We are reclaimed. We are repossessed. I know that last one has some negative connotations to it. But it's true. When something is repo'd, new ownership has been taken. When God calls us redeemed that means there is new ownership taken. We are a new creation. We have become submissive to God to direct our path. Because you are a new creation, you are not a product of what happened to you. There's no mess too big for God to clean up because you have been Redeemed, Rescued, Recovered, Reclaimed and Repossessed. They all mean the same thing. They all say in one way or another we have been redeemed.

God calls us redeemed and God has Redeemed, Rescued, Recovered, Reclaimed and Repossessed you and exalted you to new ownership. No, God doesn't own you, but he created you and because you are redeemed you have taken new ownership over your life, over your identity. You have begun to find your identity in Christ, to be redeemed means that you were once a sinner, but you've been reclaimed by God. That's why this is the last chapter of what God calls you, because it's one of the most important. It's time we've learned all the things God has to say about us. It's time to reclaim your identity from whatever you have put it in. Whatever baskets you have placed your imaginary identity eggs in, it's time to reclaim them and place them in Jesus' basket. So, what does the Bible say about being redeemed?

> *"I have swept away your offenses like a cloud, your sins like the morning mist. Return to me, for I have redeemed you."*
> Isaiah 44:22 NIV

IT'S A CELEBRATION OF GOD'S MERCY REACHING THE HEARTS OF THOSE SOCIETY HAD REJECTED.

Return to me, for I have redeemed you. I can't help but think about Matthew in this instance. A tax collector, a Jewish tax collector, stealing from his own people. He was considered the lowest of the low to his people. But Jesus saw greatness in him, he saw what God saw, he didn't see a tax collector, he didn't see a sinner, he saw a redeemed child of God. As we see in the story of Matthew, Jesus is having dinner at Matthew's house, surrounded by other tax collectors and sinners. The religious leaders questioned this, but Jesus, in His wisdom, explained that He came for the spiritually sick. This gathering was a feast of redemption, a celebration of God's mercy reaching the hearts of those society had rejected. Through this, Jesus emphasized the essence of His mission to call sinners to repentance and offer them new life, a new identity. We can no longer identify with something of the past for we are new creations. We are repossessed under new ownership, our past no longer has a stronghold on us. Matthew experienced this first hand walking with Jesus. Not only was his identity transformed but he got to watch the identities of many others be transformed by Jesus. In every life-changing moment the disciples got to witness identities were rescued and not abandoned.

> *"Jesus gave his life for our sins, just as God our Father planned, in order to rescue us from this evil world in which we live." Galatians 1:4 NLT*

Jesus' life was one of perfection all with one plan in mind, rescue all of God's children from our sins. It is no longer us who live but Christ who lives in us. We are new creations, we are redeemed, we are rescued. Just like Lazarus, Jesus brought us back to life.

THE ENEMY THOUGHT HE HAD ME

> *"He reached down from on high and took hold of me; he drew me out of deep waters. He rescued me from my powerful enemy,*

from my foes, who were too strong for me. They confronted me in the day of my disaster, but the Lord was my support. He brought me out into a spacious place; he rescued me because he delighted in me." Psalm 18:16-19 NIV

The psalmist beautifully illustrates the nature of God's rescue. In scripture above, we see God reaching down, taking hold of us, and drawing us out of deep waters. When the enemy thinks he has us, God intervenes. It's a reminder that our rescue is not dependent on our strength but on the unwavering might of our Heavenly Father. As we trust in God's unfailing rescue, He not only delivers us from the clutches of the enemy but also brings us into a spacious place. This spacious place is a metaphor for God's blessings, grace, and abundance that await us beyond the trials. The enemy's plans may be for our destruction, but God's plans are for our welfare and a future filled with hope.

WHEN THE ENEMY THINKS HE HAS US, GOD INTERVENES.

Life often presents us with challenges that seem too great for us to conquer. There are moments when the enemy thinks he has us in his grasp. Yet, as believers, we find hope and strength in the realization that God always has other plans. Life is filled with unexpected challenges. It could be a health crisis, a financial struggle, or a relationship breakdown. These moments may seem like the enemy is prevailing, attempting to convince us that we are defeated. But, as we navigate through these difficulties, let us remember that God's plans for our lives go beyond the schemes of the enemy.

The enemy thinks he is cunning and deceptive simply because he was able to deceive Eve in the garden, but the truth is he won that battle because she did not yet have an identity. The Bible refers to her as the woman until Adam names her. So many who have an encounter with God throughout the Bible have their name changed or I would like to believe they have an identity change. Jacob became Israel, Simon became Peter and Saul became Paul. The enemy has no new plans, he will always try to attack your integrity and your identity with fear, doubt and lies. But you have been redeemed, remember that next time the enemy tries to attack your identity.

In the face of adversity, let us hold on to the truth that the enemy's temporary victories are no match for God's eternal plans. Even when the enemy thinks he has us, God has other plans—a plan of redemption, restoration, and victory.

IT'S ALL ABOUT THE REPO MAN

Looking at God as the Repo man is a tough sell for most people. It may sound unconventional to some, and to some even heretical, but before you start calling me a heretic let me explain. As we dive into scripture on a daily basis, we discover a loving and merciful God who reclaims and restores what rightfully belongs to Him. Everything in creation belongs to God because he created it, I know spoiler alert. Our lives, our talents, our relationships are all gifts from the Creator. However, sin entered the world, leading to a separation between God and us. God works tirelessly to reclaim and redeem what is His. Not out of harsh judgment but out of an overwhelming desire to restore us to our true identity and purpose.

> *"I will give you a new heart and put a new spirit in you; I will remove from you your heart of stone and give you a heart of flesh. And I will put my Spirit in you and move you to follow my decrees and be careful to keep my laws."*
> *Ezekiel 36:26-27 NIV*

God's repossession process is not forceful or oppressive but rather a gentle and transformative work. The Scripture from Ezekiel speaks of God giving us a new heart and a new spirit. God's repossession involves the removal of a heart of stone, symbolizing hardness and resistance, and the implantation of a heart of flesh, representing a heart softened and receptive to God's love and guidance. Unlike our repo men who may act out of necessity or legal obligation, God reclaims what is His out of boundless love. It is a love that seeks to redeem, to heal, and to bring us back into a harmonious relationship with Him.

In every repossession, God sees the potential for restoration and transformation. A repo by God is not the end but the beginning of a journey toward restoration and redemption. When God redeems our lives, He brings healing, forgiveness, and a fresh start. The Holy Spirit is given to move us towards a life that aligns with God's decrees and laws, guiding us into a closer, more intimate relationship with our Creator.

WHY DO I MATTER?

God calls you redeemed, now we had some fun in this chapter like we have in all of them. But the truth here is this. You have been redeemed. You have been rescued and not abandoned. We need to trust that God's love and mercy is enough for us. He reclaims what is rightfully His, not to condemn but to restore. While reading this, if you feel God's gentle repossession in your life, embrace it with hope and anticipation, knowing that it is the precursor to His life-changing work. You matter because He calls you redeemed.

REFLECTION

How does it feel to know you are redeemed? That you are Rescued and Not Abandoned!

_____

_____

_____

_____

_____

_____

_____

_____

CHAPTER TWELVE

Why Do I Matter?

The whole book culminates into this chapter. So, why do you matter? I've spent the last three years working on this book, it's changed over time but ultimately its concept has stayed the same. In order to find your identity in Christ you must first understand all of the things He calls you. Because, when you understand that, it helps you learn why he left the ninety-nine to find the one. Why the prodigal son was welcomed with open arms. It has nothing to do with what you do, but all about what He calls you. That's what's important. That's what we need to hold onto in the dark moments, in the silence, in the midst of tragedy and trials. If we hold onto what He calls us, we hold onto our identity in Him no matter what's going on around us. So, let's recap shall we? He calls us adopted, loved, friend (every time I

127

WHY DO I MATTER?

think of God calling me friend I sing "I am a friend of God" it just hits different. Be honest you just sang it), masterpiece, created, fearfully and wonderfully made, gifted, heir, redeemed, forgiven, and free. If He calls us all those things and all of those things are good, how can we view ourselves as anything other than good.

GOOD FOR YOU, GOOD FOR ME

Let's dive into the real deal, how God's goodness is like the superhero cape for our identities. Think about it like this: when you believe in God and believe everything He calls you and who practically has goodness as His middle name, it changes everything about how you see yourself. So, good for you and good for me right? If God's good, and He made you, that means you're pretty awesome by default. It's like getting a stamp of approval from the coolest Creator ever. Psalm 139:14 puts it like this:

> "I praise you because I am fearfully and wonderfully made; your works are wonderful, I know that full well."
> Psalm 139:14 NIV

GOD'S GOODNESS IS LIKE THE SUPERHERO CAPE FOR OUR IDENTITIES.

You're not just a random sketch; you're a masterpiece. Here comes the superhero part we discussed earlier and its non-other than Jesus. Ever heard the saying 'new and improved'? Well, that's you in Christ. When Jesus did His superhero move on the cross, it wasn't just about forgiving your mess-ups. It was like hitting the reset button on your identity. Paul, in his letter to the Corinthians, spills the beans:

"Therefore, if anyone is in Christ, the new creation has come: The old has gone, the new is here!" 2 Corinthians 5:17 NIV.

It's a total makeover, and God's goodness is the stylist. What if we picture life as a maze, and you're navigating through it. Trusting in God's goodness is like having the ultimate GPS. Proverbs 3:5-6 sums it up like this:

"Trust in the Lord with all your heart and lean not on your own understanding; in all your ways submit to him, and he will make your paths straight." Proverbs 3:5-6 NIV

God's goodness becomes your compass, helping you find your way through twists and turns. When life throws lemons, you're making some serious lemonade, all because of the goodness of God. Let's be real, life isn't all rainbows, unicorns and sunshine. But here's the thing: God's goodness doesn't just shine when everything's perfect; it's the flashlight in the dark. Romans 8:28 says:

"And we know that in all things God works for the good of those who love him, who have been called according to his purpose." Romans 8:28 NIV

It's like God's taking all the messy bits and turning them into something good. Your scars? They're proof of a story where God's goodness always wins. Imagine your identity as something contagious. Being soaked in the goodness of God means you will spill out overflowing onto everyone around you. If your identity is wrapped up in God's goodness, it becomes a love bomb that explodes over everyone nearby.

LOVE BOMB

Can we talk about the cosmic, out-of-this-world, can't-be-contained kind of love for a minute? God's love. Love isn't just a warm fuzzy feeling; it's one of the main ingredients that creates our identity found in Christ. Imagine God writing you a love note, not on paper but in your very existence. If God is love (1 John 4:8), then your identity is basically a love letter written in the stars. You're not some random doodle; you're a masterpiece crafted with love. Your quirks, your talents, even your goof-ups, they're all part of this love story. Ever feel like you're a puzzle missing a few pieces? Well, God's love is the missing link. It's not just a pat on the back; it's a warm embrace that says, "You're mine." Ephesians 2:8-9 breaks it down for us:

> *"For it is by grace you have been saved, through faith—*
> *and this is not from yourselves, it is the gift of God—not*
> *by works, so that no one can boast." Ephesians 2:8-9 NIV*

You're not earning brownie points; you're living in a love that's freely given. Not freely given in fear or angst but freely given. God's love isn't just a one-way street. It's an invitation to a party where you're not just a guest but a VIP.

"Dear friends, since God so loved us, we also ought to love one another." 1 John 4:11 NIV

Your identity isn't just about being loved; it's about spreading it and not just love but kindness, forgiveness, and compassion until it becomes contagious. Love is the star of the show. So, let your identity dance to the rhythm of God's love. It's not just a beat; it's the heartbeat of who you are. You're not just living; you're living loved. So, grab a front-row seat, soak in God's love, and let the world see an identity that's rooted, defined, and beautifully tangled in Jesus.

YOU CAN'T HANDLE THE TRUTH

Some people can and some people can't, they say the truth hurts. In this case though, God's truth isn't just facts and figures; it's the GPS guiding us through the twists and turns of our journey into finding our identity. Ever wonder why you're wired a certain way? Well, God's truth is the blueprint of your design. It's not about fitting into some cookie-cutter mold; it's about discovering your unique thumbprint in the grand design.

"For you created my inmost being; you knit me together in my mother's womb. I praise you because I am fearfully and wonderfully made; your works are wonderful, I know that full well." Psalm 139:13-14 NIV

Your identity isn't a draft; it's a masterpiece, designed with truth as the guiding principle. In a world of fake news and

Photoshop, God's truth stands as the anchor. It's not about being flawless; it's about being real. God's truth isn't about perfection; it's about love and faithfulness. Your identity isn't a cover story; it's a story all about the truth. Now, have you ever had that voice in your head saying you're not good enough? That's negative self-talk that doesn't belong to God or His truth about you.

> *"Then you will know the truth, and the truth will set you free."*
> *John 8:32 NIV*

TRUSTING IN GOD'S GOODNESS IS LIKE HAVING THE ULTIMATE GPS.

Your identity isn't shaped by lies; it's set free by the truth. You're not chained; because as the joke "why can't Jesus wear jewelry" goes, Jesus breaks every chain. This isn't just a plot twist; it's the narrative thread woven into every chapter of this book. So, let your identity be a story of truth, not fiction. You're not just living; you're living out the truth. Grab that truth torch, light up the path. Because the fact of the matter is your identity in Jesus is found in his truth.

SO, WHY DOES THIS ALL MATTER ANYWAY?

You matter, that's plain and simple. Ok the end...That would be a fun way to end it wouldn't it? It matters because you matter, you matter to me, to your family, to your friends. You matter! Most importantly though. You matter to God. God's goodness, His love, and His truth all matter to you and everyone around you. You see these principles we've discussed, all of this stuff that God calls you, it's all intertwined in the stars above. It's part of the greatest love story the galaxy has ever seen. You matter that much to God. He gave you qualities unique to you that no one in this world could ever have. He calls us Adopted, Loved, Friend, Masterpiece, Created, Fearfully and Wonderfully Made, Gifted, Heir, Redeemed, Forgiven, and Free. All of those things can be wrapped up in what we talked about in this chapter, Gods goodness, Gods love, and Gods truth. Your identity in Christ is so much more than what you look like or what you do. It's all about what God calls you.

REFLECTION

Now, after reading this book, I want you to list all the reasons you believe you matter.

_____

_____

_____

_____

_____

_____

_____

_____

_____

ABOUT
JOSHUA DAVIES

*O*osh is passionate about seeing others come to know Jesus. Not only come to know Jesus but understand who they are in Him and who He calls them to be. He and his wife pour their heart and soul into a community they love and long to see people come to know Jesus. Putting their passion into every aspect of family and ministry.

Josh and his wife, Whitney, have been serving as Co-Lead pastors at New Life since August of 2022. Josh has been licensed with the Assemblies of God since 2017. He has an undergrad degree in Digital Media and Communications from University of Valley Forge. God called him to step into ministry along side of his wife in 2015 when she was a children's pastor in Gillette, WY. He has served as church planter and worship pastor, along with many other various ministries within the church. Josh and Whitney have 3 beautiful daughters who love to serve the church and community right alongside of mom and dad.

mynesso.com/PastorJoshDavies

Made in the USA
Monee, IL
02 August 2024

62831079R00075